TABLE OF CONTENTS

Fifties Blondes

SEXBOMBS, SIRENS, BAD GIRLS AND TEEN QUEENS

RICHARD KOPER

Published in the USA by:
BearManor Media
P. O. Box 71426
Albany, GA 31708
www.bearmanormedia.com

ISBN 978-1-59393-521-4

Printed in the United States of America
Book design by Brian Pearce | Red Jacket Press

For Yannique

CLEO MOORE

ACKNOWLEDGEMENTS

First of all, I'd like to make a special note of gratitude to my parents who have supported me through all those years of collecting. Thanks, Dad, for taking me to Amsterdam and buying my first Marilyn Monroe book twenty-five years ago! I'd also like to thank my sister, family and all my friends who patiently accepted my addiction all these years; listening to me being ecstatic, when I just found a new photograph, poster or magazine at a film fair. (That was part of the excitement of collecting before the coming of the Internet!) I appreciate your support and interest in all these years of my collecting and while I was working on this book.

About 95% of the photo material in this book is from my own collection. The other 5% are from the huge collection of my collector friend, Robert Rotter. Thanks, Rob, for letting me use some of your great stills for this project.

Finally, I like to say thanks to Ben Ohmart, publisher of BearManor Media. Thank you for believing in this subject and for putting it in print.

SABRINA

INTRODUCTION

What started my fascination with fifties movie blondes? I remember watching *Some Like it Hot* when I was twelve years old. I was struck by the character of Sugar Kane; of course, played by blonde Marilyn Monroe. I started collecting newspaper and magazine clippings of her. Since it was exactly twenty years after her mysterious death at the time, there were a lot of publications in the press and documentaries on television. I bought my first Marilyn Monroe biography (John Kobal's *Marilyn Monroe*) and learned from that book that she had a lot of impersonators in her time. I joined the Dutch Marilyn Monroe fan club, bought more books, and watched late night movies on the German television with Marilyn, Beverly Michaels and Mamie Van Doren (they all were synchronized with German voices!). In 1984, my collection mostly consisted of magazine clippings and videotaped films. When British blonde Diana Dors died that year, I learned she had her own copycat following in Britain during her peak of fame. Gradually, my list of American and English blonde sex-bombs grew and grew. I regularly went to the two vintage movie shops Amsterdam had and visited film fairs where I bought some great stills, magazines and lobby cards (after hours of searching piles of photos, posters, etc.). In 1990, I went to New York for a vacation, destined to come back with some nice memorabilia. And I succeeded! (I only wished I had more to spend these days!) With the coming of the Internet my collection grew dynamically. I now even have items I didn't dare to hope for in the beginning of my collecting years. My dream was to make this book, to share my collection and information with those interested all over the world. Although my photo collection was big enough to fill a book, I needed more specific information about the lives and careers of these women. Searching the Internet, browsing casting lists and star biographies, and spending a whole day at the New York library during my second New York visit, gave me a lot of information about birth dates, real names, film credits, etc. Through all these years I can now say I have some solid information for this book; any missing information about these ladies known to my readers is welcome to me (you can contact me at *fiftiesblondes@hotmail.com*). I do not claim to be complete in my listings of fifties blondes. Included in this book are:

Movie stars and starlets who have been called Marilyn Monroe competitors or imitators somewhere in their career.

Sexy blondes who made a career in B-movies, from Westerns to the teenage-genre.

Actresses who turned blonde during their movie career and got sexier roles because of this hair/color change.

In an appendix called "Other Fifties Blondes," I have listed 46 sexy Hollywood and British blondes who were also big names, sexy starlets or glamour girls, but who are not the main focus of my collecting. But not mentioning them, though, would make this book less complete. To draw a line, I only included blondes that were born between 1922 and 1938, and had played in films in the US or UK in the 1950s and/or early 1960s. (That means, for example, that Marie McDonald and June Haver, who were born in 1923 and 1926 respectively, but starred in movies in the 1940s, are not included in this book. However, promising MGM starlet Lila Leeds, who became infamous when she was arrested smoking marihuana with Robert Mitchum and found her career over, is included because I've ranked her among her fellow forties starlets who made somewhat of a name for themselves in the early fifties. A couple European actresses (e.g., French Mylène Demongeot) are included in the appendix, because they appeared in some sexy blonde roles in US or UK productions.

I hope you will enjoy the contents of this book as much as I do collecting these fabulous fifties blondes!

Richard Koper
Holland
April 9, 2008

Fifties Blondes

MAMIE VAN DOREN

Gentlemen Prefer Blondes: the famous title of the movie that gave super stardom to the ultimate fifties blonde bombshell, Marilyn Monroe. But why do men prefer blondes? Maybe because blonde is associated with sex, fun and carelessness? "Blondes have more fun" was another catchy phrase in the fifties. Blondes are girls that can give you a good time, without expecting much in return. And, as the former quote implies, they're also having a good time for their own pleasure! In the forties and fifties a woman was brought up to have one goal in life: to please her husband in marriage. Maybe that idea gave way to the belief that being blonde was synonymous to being a floozy. These stereotyped *femme fatales* have been around since Hollywood started making films. But it was in the fifties that film producers started to advertise their productions with more explicit sexuality. Many movie posters promised more than the actual movie showed. British *Picturegoer* magazine noted on this: "You know the sort of posters I'm talking about. The provocative blonde sprawling enticingly across a hoarding…the half-shadowed, half-naked girl beckoning…the balloon-like figures that distend a star's figure disgustingly."[1] Fifties producers and studios had to compete with two strong forces to keep the audience coming to the cinemas. First there was the fast-growing medium of television. And secondly the artificial Hollywood bombshells got competition from a more natural, sexy star. These "new women" came from Europe. Especially the Scandinavian and the French productions, with blonde sex kitten Brigitte Bardot attracting many American men that wanted to see more on screen than the US censors allowed. As Paula Yates wrote in her *Blondes* book: "Blondes will always seem unthreatening to men, who continue to act as if the most determinedly calculating blonde will inevitably become a dizzy sex kitten, be putty in his hunky hand. The blonde, of course, realized the minute she took the big step towards being a real pretend blonde that a whole world of blondeness opens up. A world of getting away with it…"[2]

1. "Clean up your posters" by Burt Rainer. *Picturegoer* magazine, July 28, 1956.

2. *"Blondes – A history from their earliest roots"* by Paula Yates. Published by Michael Joseph Ltd. 1983, Great Britain.

Hollywood blondes have been of all eras. During the twentieth century, the most well-known blondes were represented almost entirely by movie stars. During the golden age of Hollywood there were independent girls who laughed at sex. These 1930s blondes were represented by big names like Jean Harlow, Mae West and starlets like Toby Wing. These ladies were glamorous, funny, naughty and sexy. The Depression made the movies a dream world to escape the sorrows of real life. The Hays' Production Code was on its way, but before it censored Hollywood, the actresses were allowed to show skin and make fun of sex. The forties marked an era of soberness and war. In the forties, while men were on the warfront, the women back home were transformed into seductresses (Veronica Lake and Lana Turner), girls next door (Betty Grable and June Haver) and comediennes (Betty Hutton and Marie Wilson). Many B-musicals, Westerns or comedies featured its own blonde lead (Adele Jergens, Marion Martin or Janis Carter).

But it was the fifties that was *the* era of the blonde bombshell. The Second World War had ended. Americans had better living standards than elsewhere in the world. Everything went bigger, bolder and better. That was also the case in Hollywood. "The Fifties blonde was the girl to match the new utopia that post-war America was aspiring to. She was artificial and bigger than anything that had gone before, in every area of her anatomy except her brain."[3] CinemaScope made movies and their stars huge and colorful. 3-D was an invention of the fifties. A lot of the movie action was tongue in cheek, but the ladies themselves were bigger than ever. The fifties blondes were consistently cast in roles that exploited their sex appeal. This system of typecasting meant that the same actress played the same type of role in every picture. Dumb blonde parts went to Marilyn Monroe and Jayne Mansfield. Most of the time they were not aware of their physique. The dumb blondes were innocent minded girls who were willing and eager to please a man. Sharp-tongued blondes like Barbara Nichols filled in the co-starring roles, making the audience laugh at their wisecracking remarks. The bad girls and "other women" (e.g., Cleo Moore and Beverly Michaels) were scheming mistresses who went for romance but, foremost…money! The fifties also was a decade for a totally new genre: The teenage movie. Stars like Mamie Van Doren, June Kenney and Yvonne Lime played troubled teenagers in conflict with boys, parents or the law. And then there were the starlets. Dozens a month arrived in Hollywood hoping to grab a chance of luck in the movie business. The most of them modeled their image after then-famous stars. They adopted the originators' techniques, adjusted them to their own needs, and often achieved varying degrees of success. Not only was glamour a big aspect in pictures in the United States, but in Europe producers and film studios were in search of their own

3. *"Blondes – A history from their earliest roots"* by Paula Yates. Published by Michael Joseph Ltd. 1983, Great Britain.

(blonde) glamorous leading ladies. Italy stayed natural with the brunette charms of Sophia Loren, Silvana Pampanini and Gina Lollobrigida, the French preferred the charms of blondes like Martine Carol, Dora Doll and Brigitte Bardot and in Great Britain reigning blonde movie queen Diana Dors had her own blonde following, with starlets like Sabrina, Vera Day and Jill Adams.

This book is about the blondes who appeared in US and UK movies during the fifties. They represented an era of glitter and glamour and, above anything, innocence. All padded up for "The Battle of the Bust," they fought for recognition and fame. Some succeeded, most failed. 100 blondes who are fondly remembered by fifties glamour girl fans are featured within the pages of this book. Enjoy!

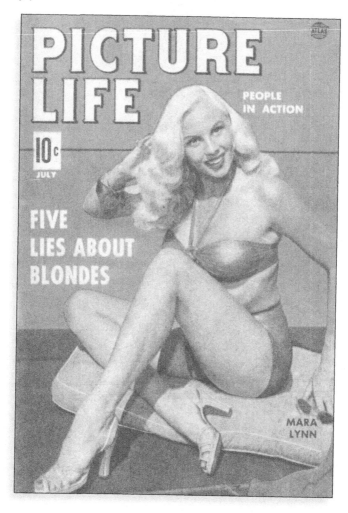

Jill Adams

Brown-eyed Jill Adams launched herself a lot of publicity early in her career, due to a stunt which promoted her as "The British Marilyn Monroe." She was born as Jill Siggins in London, but raised in New Zealand, on July 20, 1930, the daughter of a New Zealand father and an American mother. At age seven the family returned to the United Kingdom. Before entering show business, she earned a living as a shop girl, secretary, window dresser, and model and even worked as a farmhand for four years in North Wales. She also appeared in advertising films in this period. Her first marriage, to James Adams, an American sailor, was dissolved in 1953. The couple had married in 1951 and from that marriage a daughter, Robertina, was born in 1952. In 1953, 200 models, including Jill, paraded in a London ballroom for a chance to appear as extras in King Arthur's court scenes in *The Black Knight*. When the film's producers and director looked the girls over, among the first one they picked was Jill Adams. More movies soon followed and her parts grew substantially. It happened while she was making *The Young Lovers* in 1954. The Pinewood studio publicity department asked her to wear a dress four sizes too small, shot photographs and exclaimed: "This is Britain's answer to Marilyn Monroe!" The stunt worked. Jill got headlines in the press, the papers were full of pin-up pictures of her and soldiers in the Middle East voted her their favourite glamour girl (in preference to Marilyn Monroe and Jane Russell). Rank studios picked her up and she signed a contract with them in 1955. Among the movies she made at Rank were two comedies with glamour girls Brigitte Bardot and Diana Dors. In the first one, *Doctor at Sea*, she played the captain's daughter who tries to seduce doctor Dirk Bogarde. The latter, *Value for Money*, had her cast as a showgirl. Due to expected rivalry between Miss Dors and Jill Adams, she received a lot of press coverage. But the two actresses got along fine and were seen chatting friendly together during breaks. It was around this time that she realized the Monroe gag was misfiring: "A second Marilyn? I don't want to be a second anybody. I want to be the first Jill Adams," she said. Complaining that people wouldn't take her seriously as an actress, she said, "They're all too keen on my shape." She left Rank and her agent landed her some good parts in quality movies like

THE YOUNG LOVERS, 1954 (GENERAL FILM DISTRIBUTORS).

WITH DIRK BOGARDE IN *DOCTOR AT SEA*, 1955 (RANK).

Private's Progress (1956), a satire about British army life with Richard Attenborough and Ian Carmichael (she's the only girl in the cast); a comedy about solicitors Alastair Sim and George Cole, *The Green Man* (1956), and a drama called *The Scamp* (1957), again with Attenborough, had her cast in a good part as the neglecting stepmother of Colin Petersen. *Picturegoer* magazine wrote in its review: "Jill Adams is briefly impressive as (Terence) Morgan's kind, brassy

WITH DIANA DORS AND JOHN GREGSON IN *VALUE FOR MONEY*, 1955 (RANK).

seconde wife." With her new star status, Jill was often quoted in the press. For example, about British film studios and their attitude toward sex: "Afraid of sex? They don't even know it exists!" and about her many pin-up poses: "We've got some very good retouchers, you know!" She also starred in a television movie called *Wideawake* that year. But her success wasn't everlasting. In 1957 she complained to *Picturegoer* magazine that not one film producer seemed willing to employ her: "I haven't made a film since August. I'm beginning to think producers have put an embargo on me." In the same article she suggested she would go to Australia to find work there. (A remarkable suggestion since Australia's small film business was most unlikely to give her career a boost.) But in 1958 she did go Down Under; taking her second husband, newscaster Peter Haigh, and daughter Robertina with her. She even got herself a role in a movie called *Dust in the Sun* and appeared on Australian television in the adventure series *The Flying Doctor*. In it she played the part of Nurse Mary Meredith. The

PUBLICITY STILL FOR TV'S *THE FLYING DOCTOR*, WITH ALAN WHITE AND
RICHARD DENNING, 1959.

WITH DENNIS PRICE IN *PRIVATE'S PROGRESS*, 1956 (BRITISH LION).

doctor of the title was played by American actor Richard Denning. The series proved to be very successful, also outside Australia. But this success didn't do much for her film career. In lack of other film roles she returned to Britain in 1959, starting all over in minor roles in two *Carry On* comedies. Jill Adams had one last starring role, in a small film called *Crosstrap*, which was completed late 1961 and released in January 1962. After a couple of small roles in some good movies, she retired from the movie business in 1965. In 1976 she divorced husband Peter Haigh after 20 years of marriage. Shortly after her divorce, she moved to the Algarve, Portugal. Back in 1956 she commented on why she was in the movies: "I'm in them because this is the most lucrative job I had so far!" Jill Adams died on May 13, 2008 in Clareance, Portugal.

JILL ADAMS FILMOGRAPHY

1953: *The Case of the Bogus Count.*

1954: *Forbidden Cargo* (dancing partner of Nigel Patrick), *The Black Knight*, *The Young Lovers* (Judy).

1955: *Out of the Clouds*, The *Love Match* (Clarrie), *One Jump Ahead* (Judy), *The Constant Husband* (Miss Brent), *Doctor at Sea* (Jill), *Value for Money* (Joy), *One Way Out* (Shirley Harcourt).

1956: *Private's Progress* (Prudence Greenslade), *The Green Man* (Ann Vincent), *Count of Twelve.*

1957: *Brothers in Law* (Sally Smith), *The Scamp* (Julie Dawson).

1958: *Death Over My Shoulder* (Evelyn Connors), *Dust in the Sun.*

1959: *Carry On Nurse* (nurse).

1960: *Carry On Constable* (Policewoman Harrison).

1962: *Crosstrap* (Sally).

1963: *Doctor in Distress* (Genevieve), *The Yellow Teddybears* (June Wilson), *The Comedy Man* (Jan Kennedy).

1965: *Promise Her Anything* (Mrs. Van Crispin).

VIOLENT ROAD, 1958 (WARNER BROS.)

Merry Anders

    Certainly one of the busiest and most versatile blonde actresses of the fifties, green-eyed Merry Anders graced many B-movies and television shows. From thrillers to comedies, from Westerns to juvenile delinquent movies, Merry made the most of her many film roles. She was born Merry Helen Anderson, on May 22, 1934, in Chicago, Illinois. When she and her mother Helen visited Los Angeles in 1949, their two-week stay became a permanent one. Merry started modeling while still a teenager and, due to her success as a model, she was signed to a starlet contract at 20th Century-Fox in 1951. She played minor roles in some high-profile movies like *Les Misérables* (1952) and *Titanic* (1953), but in 1954 her contract wasn't renewed. Merry wasn't out of work for long. She did a lot of television work and had a couple of movie parts. She joined the cast of *The Stu Erwin Show* in 1954 and was a regular on CBS comedy *It's Always Jan* (1955-56). In it she played a shapely blonde model named Valerie Malone, who shares a Manhattan apartment with nightclub entertainer Janis Paige and secretary Patricia Bright. On March 25, 1955, Merry married casting director John Stephens. Within six months the marriage fell apart; a divorce was granted in September 1955. In the middle of the divorce, Merry learned that she was pregnant. In 1956 she gave birth to a daughter, Tina Beth Paige Anders. Although one would assume that being a single young mother would keep someone busy, Merry started to tour the west coast in the play *Will Success Spoil Rock Hunter?* in 1956. (When Jayne Mansfield left the play on Broadway, Merry stepped in her footsteps as screen star Rita Marlowe.) Following this play, Merry proved to be quite busy. In 1957 she appeared in seven movies and worked on television in *How to Marry a Millionaire*, which ran until 1959, based on the Marilyn Monroe movie of the same title. A much publicized movie role was that of Ruth Collins in Paramount's *Hear Me Good*. Her famous "shrinking dress" scene got her a lot of press coverage. In this period Merry's hair color changed from brunette to blonde, varying with the roles she played. As a brunette she was seen in the small musical film *Calypso Heatwave*; a film about drug abuse, *Death in Small Doses*, and she took part in an all-girl Western called *The Dalton Girls* (although a brunette in the movie, Merry was blonde in all publicity photos!). Together with sisters

HEAR ME GOOD, 1957 (PARAMOUNT).

Penny Edwards, Lisa Davis and Sue George, she carried on the violent family tradition. In a final shoot-out Holly loses her life. After this busy year Merry made only one movie in 1958. In 1960 she starred in the low-budget Western *Five Bold Women*, with fellow blondes Irish McCalla and Kathy Marlowe. She later commented that most of the female cast was harassed by the male crew. Only Irish McCalla and she didn't give in to the men. In the 1960s Merry played in a

WITH CHARLOTTE AUSTIN AND BETTY GRABLE IN *HOW TO MARRY A MILLIONAIRE*, 1953 (20TH CENTURY FOX).

string of B-movies, with titles like: *20,000 Eyes* (1961), *The Case of Patty Smith* (1962), a then-daring movie about abortion, and the chiller *House of the Damned* (1963). The sixties were rounded out with an Elvis Presley movie called *Tickle Me* (1965), for which Merry had to gain a lot of weight, and a terrible science fiction movie called *Women of the Prehistoric Planet* (1966), which is not to be confused with Mamie Van Doren's awful *Voyage to the Planet of Prehistoric Women*, released that same year. For the television series *Dragnet 1967* (which ran from 1967 'til 1970), Jack Webb insisted that she wear a brunette wig. After a cameo appearance in blockbuster movie *Airport* (1970) and a starring role in *Legacy of Blood* (1971), Merry quit acting to live "a normal life," as she stated in a *FilmFax* interview. Thirty-one years after her divorce from John Stephens, she married Litton engineer Richard Benedict. She became a customer relations coordinator at Litton Data Systems Industries and retired in 1994.

THE DALTON GIRLS, 1957 (UNITED ARTISTS).

WITH DONA DRAKE AND DEBRA PAGET IN *PRINCESS OF THE NILE*, 1954 (20TH CENTURY FOX).

WITH BRIAN KEITH IN *VIOLENT ROAD*, 1958 (WARNER BROS.).

LOBBY CARD FOR *NO TIME TO BE YOUNG*, 1957 (COLUMBIA).

WITH RON FOSTER IN *THE WALKING TARGET*, 1960 (UNITED ARTISTS).

1951: *Golden Girl* (chorine).

1952: *Belles on Their Toes* (student). *Wait 'til the Sun Shines, Nellie* (Adeline Halper/Burdge), *Les Misérables* (Cicely).

1953: *Titanic* (college girl), *The Farmer Takes a Wife* (Hannah), *How to Marry a Millionaire* (model).

1954: *Princess of the Nile* (handmaiden), *Three Coins in a Fountain, Phffft!* (Marcia).

1955: *All That Heaven Allows* (Mary-Ann).

1957: *Desk Set* (Cathy), *The Night Runner* (Amy Hansen), *The Dalton Girls* (Holly Dalton), *No Time to Be Young* (Gloria Stuben), *Calypso Heatwave* (Marti Collins), *Hear Me Good* (Ruth Collins), *Escape From San Quentin* (Robbie), *Death in Small Doses* (Amy Phillips).

1958: *Violent Road* (Carrie).

1960: *Five Bold Women* (The Missouri Lady), *The Hypnotic Eye* (Dodie Wilson), *Young Jesse James* (Belle Starr), *The Walking Target* (Susan Mallory), *Police Dog Story* (Terry Payton), *Spring Affair* (Dorothy).

1961: *20,000 Eyes* (Karen Walker), *The Gambler Wore a Gun* (Sharon Donovan), *Secret of Deep Harbor* (Janey Fowler), *When the Clock Strikes* (Ellie).

1962: *Air Patrol* (Mona Whitney), *The Beauty and the Beast* (Sybil), *The Case of Patty Smith* (Mary).

1963: *House of the Damned* (Nancy Campbell), *Police Nurse* (Joan Olson).

1964: *A Tiger Walks* (Betty Collins), *FBI Code 98* (Grace McLean), *The Quick Gun* (Helen Reed), *The Time Travellers* (Carol White).

1965: *Tickle Me* (Estelle Penfield), *Raiders From Beneath the Sea* (Dottie Harper), *Young Fury* (Alice).

1966: *Women of the Prehistoric Planet* (Lt. Karen Lamont).

1967: *Flight of the Cougar* (Carol Dawson).

1970: *Airport.*

1971: *Legacy of Blood* (Laura Dean).

Roxanne Arlen

Roxanne Arlen was the starlet who made headlines in 1957 when she filed for a divorce, because her husband Tom Roddy couldn't cope with the effect her built-in wiggle had on other men! This self-selling blonde ("There's nothing wrong with being commercial if it sells," she told the press once), started out as a redhead in the early fifties on television and in small movie parts. By then she had already married (1947) and divorced (1951) famous comedian Red Buttons. She was born on January 10, 1931, in Detroit, Michigan, and moved to Los Angeles when still a child. In 1956, Roxanne and 14 other actresses were chosen as "WAMPAS Baby Stars" by a group of veteran actors and actresses. This and her own gift for self-publicity landed her a couple of movie roles like *Bundle of Joy* (1956), in which she tries to bust up the romance of Eddie Fisher and Debbie Reynolds, and *Everything But the Truth* (1956), in which she demonstrates an old man pacifier trick with the doorknob to Maureen O'Hara. She was a carhop in the teenage melodrama *The Young Stranger* (1957) and shared a scene with its lead actor, James MacArthur. A meatier role came with the little crime film *The Big Caper* (1957). She was largely publicized in all the ad material in favor of the film's female star, blonde Mary Costa. But, nonetheless, film roles stopped coming after this movie. She was seen sporadically on television and seemed forgotten by Hollywood producers. In 1958 she played a small role as the sexy dumb blonde Gloria Coogle in the Broadway play *Who Was That Lady I Saw You With?* (a role played in the movie *Who Was That Lady?* by Barbara Nichols). The play opened on March 3, 1958 and was a hit with the press and the public. Nevertheless, there were no new roles coming for Roxanne, she became depressed and tried to take her life with tranquilizers in February of 1959. Luckily for her, the 1960s brought her career new chances. She appeared regularly on television and returned to the big screen in a comic part as Mrs. Roberts in Frank Tashlin's *Bachelor Flat* (1962) and as a stripper called Electra in *Gypsy* (1962), singing "You Gotta Have a Gimmick" to Natalie Wood. In the former she is seen in the same dress Marilyn Monroe wore in the famous skirt-blowing scene from *The Seven Year Itch* (1955). At the end of the sixties she called it quits and married retailer Bill Schaffer in February 1969. It was her third and

WITH GORDON MACRAE AND SALLY TODD IN *THE BEST THINGS IN LIFE ARE FREE*, 1956 (20TH CENTURY FOX).

THE YOUNG STRANGER, 1957 (RKO).

last marriage. During the last years of her life, Arlen lived in England and wrote plays for the Oval House Theater in London. Roxanne Arlen died, at age 58, on February 22, 1989, in London.

WITH JOCK MAHONEY IN *SLIM CARTER*, **1957 (UNIVERSAL).**

ROXANNE ARLEN FILMOGRAPHY

1955: *Son of Sinbad* (raider), *Illegal* (Ginnie Hathaway), *Battle Cry* (blonde).

1956: *Miracle in the Rain* (Cathy Wicklow), *The Best Things in Life are Free* (Perky Nichols), *Everything But the Truth* (blonde), *Hot Rod Girl* (L.P.), *Bundle of Joy* (blonde on dance floor).

1957: *The Young Stranger* (carhop), *The Helen Morgan Story* (showgirl), *Slim Carter* (cigarette girl), *The Big Caper* (Doll).

1962: *Gypsy* (Electra), *Bachelor Flat* (Mrs. Roberts).

1964: *A House is Not a Home* (Hattie Miller's girl).

1965: *The Loved One* (Whispering Glades hostess).

Judy Bamber

More a model then a movie star, Judy Bamber had a short-lived career in B-movies and television shows. She was born (as Judith Lee Bamber) on October 13, 1936, in Ann Arbor, Michigan where she started modeling while still in high school. Before she modeled she had to lose a lot of weight: "In high school in Dearborn, I was very popular with the boys, but only as a pal. I wasn't very attractive and I weighed 130 pounds." After moving to Detroit, she began making appearances on local television, where she met Frank Robinson, a television announcer whom she married in 1956. He went to Hollywood to produce a movie, but the couple didn't find much success in either of their chosen careers for a long time. When her old modeling pictures were printed in a paper, she was noticed by a film agent. She attended the Warner Brothers acting school, where she met fellow student James Stacy, who helped her get a contract at Warner Bros. But her agent had been busy getting her a contract with American-International Pictures. Both studios ended up dropping her, but she did get a movie out of it, the low-budget teenage movie *Dragstrip Girl* (1957), directed by Edward L. Cahn. Judy was seen as Fay Spain's friend Rhoda, a typical dumb blonde. In *Up in Smoke* (1957) she was a waitress and gang moll in what was to be one of the last Bowery Boys movies. On television, she assisted host George Fenneman on the quiz show *Anybody Can Play* (1958). It is said that

WITH JOHN ASHLEY IN *DRAGSTRIP GIRL*, 1957 (AIP).

WITH HUNTZ HALL IN *UP IN SMOKE*, 1957 (ALLIED ARTISTS).

Alfred Hitchcock considered her for his upcoming suspense movie *Vertigo* (1958). Kim Novak eventually played the part Judy tested for. The next year Judy was the dead body under mad sculptors Dick Miller's plaster in Roger Corman's *Bucket of Blood* (1959). She was strangled with a scarf while posing for Miller in his apartment. Seen mostly on television in the sixties, Judy Bamber quit acting in 1964, to raise her two-year-old son Louis.

JUDY BAMBER FILMOGRAPHY

1957: *Young and Dangerous* (party girl), *Up in Smoke* (Mabel), *Dragstrip Girl* (Rhoda).
1959: *A Bucket of Blood* (Alice).
1964: *Monstrosity* (Bea Mullins).

Mari Blanchard

Former model Mari Blanchard (nee Mary), was born on April 13, 1927, in Long Beach, California. At the age of nine she fell victim to the paralyzing disease of polio, but by the age of twelve she was cured. In her late teens she started modeling for a Los Angeles swimsuit concern. It was around this time that she changed the 'y' in Mary for an 'i' and made her movie debut as a Copacabana chorus girl in the Carmen Miranda musical comedy *Copacabana* (1947). When she was spotted by cartoonist Al Capp, she became his inspiration for *Li'l Abner's* comic strip character Stupefyin' Jones. But it was a Kodak advertisement picturing Mari in a bubble bath that brought her to the attention of Paramount's talent scouts. She was signed to a contract by them in 1949. Mari was given only one small role, in the Bing Crosby musical *Mr. Music* (1950) and was dropped that same year. She freelanced for two years, working for RKO, MGM

and Columbia. In 1952 she received third billing in Universal-International's *Back at the Front*. As Nina, an Oriental seductress, she caught the eye of Universal executives and was signed to a long-term contract. Today, Mari is probably best remembered as Allura, "Queen of Venus" in *Abbott and Costello Go to Mars* (1953). In this comedy she had to stand competition to dozens of beautiful starlets (e.g. Gloria Pall) and Miss Universe contestants (among whom a young Anita Ekberg). In studio writings and press articles about Mari, it was almost always mentioned that she and Marilyn Monroe shared the same measurements. In late 1953 Mari screen-tested for a part in the

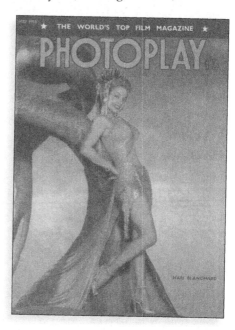

MACHETE, 1958 (UNITED ARTISTS).

upcoming Jeff Chandler adventure film, *Yankee Pasha*. Another blonde Universal hopeful, namely Mamie Van Doren, eventually landed the part. A couple of Arabian Nights tales and westerns followed, when she was released from her Universal contract in 1954. She was kept quite busy the following years starring in many low-budget movies. RKO's Technicolor production *Son of Sinbad* (1955) saw a sexy Mari in revealing costumes, while *Stagecoach to Fury* (1956)

WITH GROUCHO MARX IN *COPACABANA*, 1947 (UNITED ARTISTS).

was a period Western with Mari as a lady of a shady past. She left for Mexico to appear in a movie with Jack Kelly, *Canasta de Cuentos Mexicanos* (1956). On the casting list she was billed as Marie Blanchard. One of the films of this period that's become a kind of cult movie today is *She Devil* (1957). In this little gem she plays a terminal tubercular patient injected with an experimental serum. As a result, she's restored to perfect health. The unpleasant side effect, though, is a complete change of personality, which makes her go on a murderous crime spree. Another side-effect was her gift to change her hair color by will. In real life, Miss Blanchard also changed her hair color frequently. She was a blonde most of the time, but also appeared as a brunette in some of her movies. Republic's *No Place to Land* (1958) starred Mari as a sexy blackmailer and in United Artists' *Machete* (1958) she was the cheating, discontented wife of sugar plantation owner Albert Dekker. Then she left Hollywood for a trip to Turkey to star in a movie called

WITH DAN DURYEA IN *RAILS INTO LARAMIE*, 1954 (UNIVERSAL).

Karasu (1958). On February 14 1960, Mari married attorney Reese H. Taylor Jr. It was her first marriage, his second. Their union proved to be short-lived; the couple separated September of that very year. (Mr. Taylor apparently had a thing with blondes, because he later married blonde starlet Juli Reding.) In the early sixties, Mari made a lot of television appearances, before she returned to the

WITH FRANK LOVEJOY AND RICHARD DENNING IN *THE CROOKED WEB*, 1955 (COLUMBIA).

big screen for *Don't Knock the Twist* (1962) and *Twice Told Tales* (1963). A well-remembered television show of that period was *Klondike*. NBC broadcasted this adventure series from October 1960 until February 1961. Mari was cast as the (brunette) hotel owner Kathy O'Hara. Also in the cast were James Coburn and blonde Joi Lansing as a saloon girl. Two years later she played a saloon entertainer herself in the comedy/Western *McLintock!* (1963). This also proved to be her last movie. Mari was seen on television 'til the late 1960s. Already suffering from cancer for some years, she died on May 10 1970, survived by her second husband, photographer Vincent Conti.

NO PLACE TO LAND, 1958 (REPUBLIC).

WITH JACK KELLY IN *SHE DEVIL*, 1957 (20TH CENTURY FOX).

1947: *Copacabana* (chorus girl).

1950: *Mr. Music* (chorus girl).

1951: *On the Riviera* (Eugenie), *Bannerline* (Eloise), *No Questions Asked* (Natalie), *The Unknown Man* (Sally Tever), *Overland Telegraph* (Stella), *Ten Tall Men* (Marie DeLatour).

MEXICAN LOBBY CARD FOR *CANASTA DE CUENTOS MEXICANOS*, 1956.

1952: *The Brigand* (Dona Dolores Castro), *Assignment Paris* (Wanda Marlowe), *Something to Live For* (hat check girl), *Back at the Front* (Nina).

1953: *Abbott and Costello Go To Mars* (Queen Allura), *The Veils of Bagdad* (Selima).

1954: *Black Horse Canyon* (Alida Spain), *Rails into Laramie* (Lou Carter).

1955: *Destry* (Brandy), *Son of Sinbad* (Kristina), *The Crooked Web* (Joanie Daniel), *The Return of Jack Slade* (Texas Rose).

1956: The *Cruel Tower* (Mary "The Babe" Thompson), *Stagecoach to Fury* (Barbara Duval), *Canasta de cuentos Mexicanos*.

1957: *She Devil* (Kyra Zelas), *Jungle Heat* (Ann McRae).

1958: *No Place to Land* (Iris Lee La Vonne), *Machete* (Jean Montoya), *Karasu*.

1962: *Don't Knock the Twist* (Dulcie Corbin).

1963: *Twice Told Tales* (Sylvia), *McLintock!* (Camille).

Jeanne Carmen

Jeanne Laverne Carmon (who is of Irish-French descent) was born the youngest of twins in Paragould, Arkansas, on August 4, 1930. Fed up with her abusive stepfather and cotton picking, she ran away from home at the age of 13; eventually landing in New York City. There she appeared in two off-Broadway shows with comedian Bert Lahr, *Burlesque* (1948) and *Two on the Aisle* (1949). "I was a chorus girl, which is funny because I can't dance at all. While I was in the chorus, I was always making the wrong moves. Everybody thought I was a comedian," she recalled later. Her stage work led to modeling jobs and in the late forties she became a popular pin-up. In 1949 she married Broadway tenor/opera singer Sandy Scott. Jeanne had met him two years earlier while he was on tour with *Burlesque* in St. Louis, where Jeanne worked as a waitress at the time. Her romance with gangster Johnny Rosselli in 1950 meant the end of her marriage with Sandy Scott. Jeanne had a small part as one of the Venus Beauties in the New York-made sexploitation movie, *Striporama* (1953). Getting more serious about acting, Jeanne attended acting classes at Lee Strasberg's Actors Studio in New York. That's where she met Marilyn Monroe, with whom she kept in touch until Monroe's death in 1962. Being a trick-shot golf player besides posing for pin-ups landed her quite some publicity. Hollywood finally called in 1956. Republic Studios cast her in *The Three Outlaws*. As the sexy teen-age delinquent Lillibeth, Jeanne shared some scenes with Mamie Van Doren in *Untamed Youth* (1957). "Mamie and I weren't really friends during the making of *Untamed Youth*. All the guys were kind of ogling me, and that didn't please her." It wasn't 'til late 1957 that she changed her brunette hair color and went blonde. That same year she starred with blonde starlet Barbara Eden in the Los Angeles stage production of *Pajama Tops*. Friend and lover Errol Flynn suggested her for the role of a stripper in Warner Bros.' *Too Much, Too Soon* (1958). Most of her scene was cut out of the movie, because it was considered too hot at the time! Also in 1958, she made the movie for which she is probably best remembered: *The Monster of Piedras Blancas*. The movie was a grade-Z horror movie with some daring scenes of Jeanne undressing. "After I agreed to appear in *The Monster of Piedras Blancas*, I was offered a walk-on in a big, important

GUNS DON'T ARGUE, 1957 (VISUAL DRAMA INC.)

WITH MAMIE VAN DOREN, LORI NELSON AND JOHN RUSSELL IN *UNTAMED YOUTH*, 1957 (WARNER BROS.)

A-movie. If I had done it, I might have become a star, like Anita Ekberg or Jayne Mansfield!" Jeanne rounded out the fifties with a cameo role in *Born Reckless* (1959). In her one scene she is a rodeo girl who shares a table with Jeff Richards. But after a sing and dance performance by Mamie Van Doren, Jeanne is sitting alone again! In the late fifties she romanced Elvis Presley and Frank Sinatra, and supposedly romanced Bobby Kennedy, whom she met through

Marilyn Monroe. After Monroe's death Jeanne Carmen left Hollywood and lived in Scottsdale, Arizona. There she married a stock broker in 1963 and had three children with him. The marriage ended in divorce. Keeping her earlier life a secret to her kids, her son Brandon found a box of movie stills and magazine covers in their basement and confronted his mother. Since then Jeanne made appearances at conventions and became a familiar face in tabloids and on television again. In 2006 there were rumors that a film based on Jeanne's life was to be made with singer Christina Aguilera. (At this moment there is still nothing

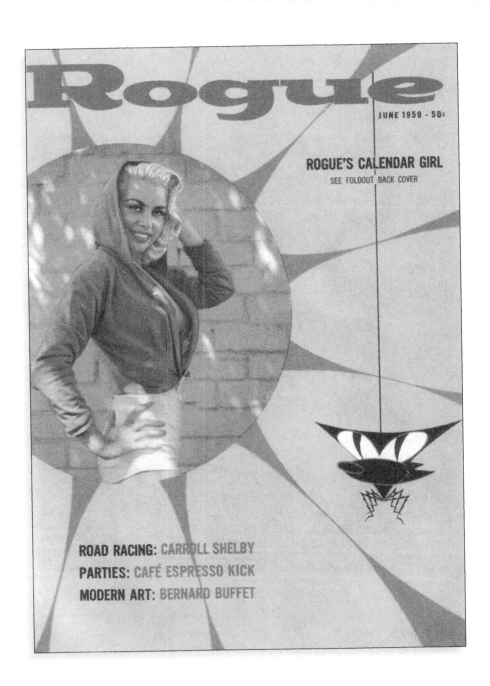

known about the realization of this production.) Her son Brandon, who wrote the filmscript of his mother's wild life story, also wrote a biography about his mother that same year. On December 20, 2007, Jeanne Carmen died from lymphoma in Irvine, California.

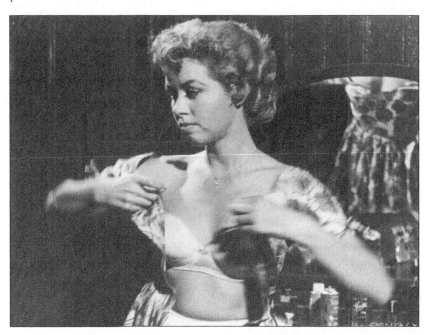

THE MONSTER OF PIEDRAS BLANCAS, 1958 (FILM SERVICE DISTRIBUTING CORPORATION).

JEANNE CARMEN FILMOGRAPHY

1954: *Striporama* (Venus beauty).
1956: *The Three Outlaws* (Serelda).
1957: *A Merry Mix-up* (Mary), *My Gun is Quick* (Café girl), *War Drums* (Yellow Moon), *Untamed Youth* (Lillibeth), *Guns Don't Argue* (Paula), *Portland Exposé* (Iris).
1958: *Too Much, Too Soon* (Tassles, a Stripper), *I Married a Woman* (blonde), *The Monster of Piedras Blancas* (Lucy).
1959: *Born Reckless* (rodeo girl).
1962: *The Devil's Hand* (blonde cultist).
1999: *Citizens of Perpetual Indulgence* (herself).
2002: *Attack of the B-Movie Monster*.
2005: *The Naked Monster* (Mrs. Lipschitz).

Marian Carr

Although Marian Carr had the looks and was a competent actress, she never reached major stardom. Marian played supporting roles in a couple of good movies, but during her career she was wasted starring in B-movie Westerns and melodramas. She was born on July 6, 1926, in Providence, Kentucky. In her early teens, Marian and her family moved to Chicago. There she attended Austin High, where she received her first stage work. After graduation she had a successful modeling career, and she was elected as "Chicago's Prettiest Office Worker" in 1946. A talent scout spotted her and she left for Hollywood to pursue an acting career. After some stage appearances, Marian was almost immediately signed by Howard Hughes. While at RKO, she appeared in two short movies, *Twin Husbands* and *Follow That Blonde* (both 1946), and played a small role in Frank Capra's classic *It's a Wonderful Life*. Then she was cast as the leading lady in the crime movie *San Quentin* (1946). In this movie she played Betty Richards, the girlfriend of an organizer of a prisoner's reform group (Lawrence Tierney), who must redeem his organization when it's threatened by an escaped killer. It was a good role in a movie that was considered brutal for its time. In 1948 Marian married Fred Levy, the head of Blum's Candy Company. The couple left Hollywood and Marian quit acting. After the birth of their son in 1952, the Levis also ended their marriage. In 1953 Marian Carr returned to Hollywood, as a single mother, and started all over again with small parts on television. In his column, reporter Erskine Johnson mentioned her with the tag line: "TV has found a new Marilyn Monroe of its own." His judgement came after viewing Marian in a part with Dick Powell in "The Witness" (1953), an episode of the *Four Star Playhouse*. She then got a part in Allied Artists' programmer *Northern Patrol* (1953). In March the following year she was granted a divorce from Mr. Levy. Robert Aldrich directed her in her next movie, *World for Ransom* (1954). Although she got special billing and looked really sexy in it, the film didn't do much for her career. Aldrich used her again in his next film, *Kiss Me Deadly* (1955). She played a mobster's sister named Friday and shared some scenes with Ralph Meeker. Although the movie received much applause, her role went unnoticed by the critics. 1955 and 1956 proved to be busy years for Marian. She appeared in a

THE DEVIL THUMBS A RIDE, 1947 (RKO).

WITH KIRBY GRANT IN *NORTHERN PATROL*, 1953 (ALLIED ARTISTS).

WITH ANTHONY CARUSO IN *WHEN GANGLAND STRIKES*, 1956 (REPUBLIC).

WITH RALPH MEEKER IN *KISS ME DEADLY*, 1955 (UNITED ARTISTS).

total of eight movies during that period. Nevertheless, she stopped acting after she played a small part in a thriller with Edward G. Robinson, *Nightmare* (1956), to focus on raising her son.

WITH WILLIAM CAMPBELL IN *CELL 2455, DEATH ROW*, 1955 (COLUMBIA).

MARIAN CARR FILMOGRAPHY

1946: *Twin Husbands* (Harriet), *Follow That Blonde, It's a Wonderful Life* (Mrs. Jane Wainwright), *San Quentin* (Betty Richards).

1947: *The Devil Thumbs a Ride* (Diane Furgeson).

1953: *Northern Patrol* (Quebec Kid).

1954: *Ring of Fear* (Valerie St. Dennis), *World for Ransom* (Frennesey March).

1955: *Kiss Me Deadly* (Friday), *Cell 2455, Death Row* (Doll), *The Seven Little Foys* (soubrette), *Ghost Town* (Barbara Leighton).

1956: *When Gangland Strikes* (Hazel), *Indestructible Man* (Eva Martin), *The Harder They Fall* (Alice), *Nightmare* (Madge Novick).

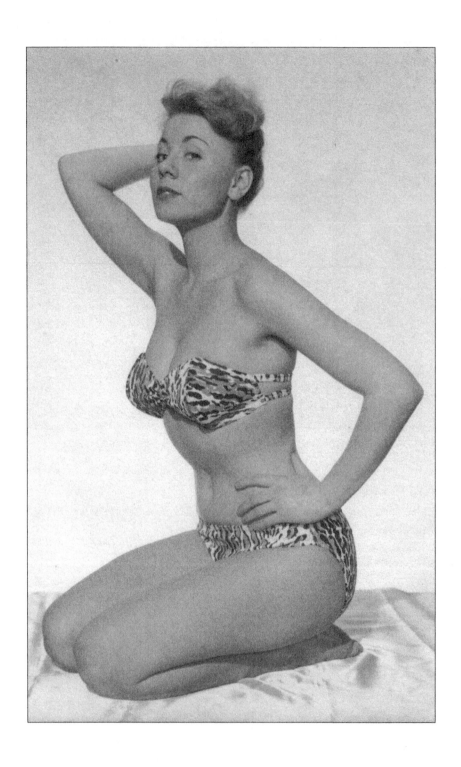

Shane Cordell

Shane Cordell was a British starlet in the mold of Diana Dors. She was born Eunice Ann Jebbett, in 1935, in Bury, Lancashire. Shane once was a telephonist at the BBC, until a meeting with an old school friend, who was a fashion model, made her try modeling herself. During her modeling days, Shane was often featured in magazines like *Spick, Span* and *Beautiful Britons.* Her movie debut was made (under her real name) in a stinker called *Fire Maidens from Outer Space* (1956), with Hollywood actor Anthony Dexter and Susan Shaw in the leading roles. Shane played one of the fire maidens. She was soon picked up

for a contract at Associated British Film Company. For them she played some small roles in comedies and was seen on television in *My Wildest Dream* (1956) and the then-popular police series *Dixon of Dock Green* (1957). In 1957 she was often referred to as "The British Jayne Mansfield," due to what the press saw as her resemblance to the American star. Unlike Miss Mansfield, however, Shane Cordell never reached major stardom and continued to play cameo roles until the late fifties.

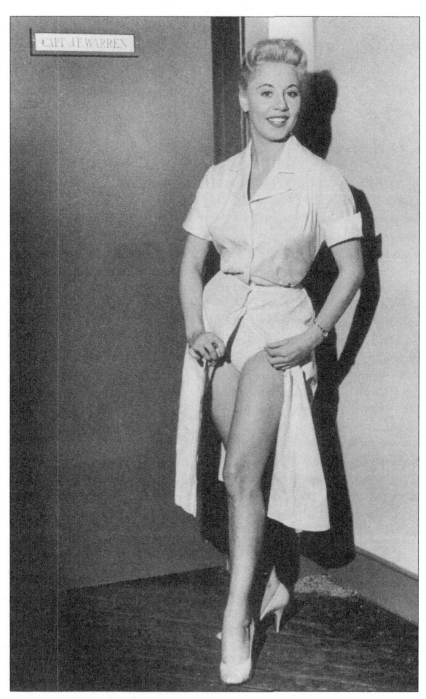

FIEND WITHOUT A FACE, 1958 (EROS/MGM).

SHANE CORDELL FILMOGRAPHY

1956: *Fire Maidens from Outer Space* (fire maiden), *The Silken Affair*, *Three Men in a Boat* (girl lover).

1957: *The Good Companions* (critic's secretary).

1958: *Girls at Sea* (bathing girl), *Fiend Without a Face* (nurse), *Bachelor of Hearts*.

1959: *Carry On Nurse* (attractive nurse).

1978: *Killer Fish* (nurse).

1983: *Frevel/Mischief.*

WITH MARIE DEVEREUX IN *GIRLS AT SEA*, 1958 (ABPC).

Dani Crayne

Dani Crayne was born Darlyne Danielle Swanson, on December 25, 1934, in Minneapolis, Minnesota. In 1951, at age 16, she married Frenchman Donalde Crayne. When Universal studios spotted her and offered her a contract she divorced Crayne (keeping his surname as her stage name). Along with Universal starlets Leigh Snowden and Mamie Van Doren, she received a big build up. She attended all kinds of classes (dancing, voice, acting) and made her debut playing the small part of an actress in *The Shrike* (1955). This was soon followed by the musical comedy *Ain't Misbehavin'* (1955). Dani played a showgirl colleague of Piper Laurie and Mamie Van Doren. More roles followed, but in 1956, due to the collapse of the Hollywood studio system, her contract wasn't renewed. She appeared on television in a *Cheyenne* episode entitled "The Iron Trail" (which aired on New Year's Day, 1957), and then was out of work for a while. Her agent got her signed to a one-year contract at Warner Bros. and she appeared in two pictures for them. In the Western *Shoot-out at Medicine Band* (1957), Angie Dickinson and Dani were the only girls in the cast. It was followed by the star-studded bomb *The Story of Mankind* (1957). After these films, Dani Crayne never made another motion picture again. Aged 30, she married singer Buddy Greco in June 1964. In 1974, this marriage ended in a divorce. A year later she married actor David Janssen, and became his widow in 1980.

DANI CRAYNE FILMOGRAPHY

1955: *The Shrike* (fluttering actress), *Ain't Misbehavin'* (Millie).
1956: *Around the World Revue, World in My Corner* (Doris), *A Day of Fury* (Claire), *The Unguarded Moment* (Josie Warren), *Written on the Wind* (blonde).
1957: *Kelly and Me* (Olive Benson), *Shoot-out at Medicine Band* (Nell Garrison), *The Story of Mankind* (Helen of Troy).

WITH RANDOLPH SCOTT IN *SHOOT-OUT AT MEDICINE BAND*, 1957 (WARNER
BROS.)

THE UNGUARDED MOMENT, 1956 (UNIVERSAL).

WITH DALE ROBERTSON IN *A DAY OF FURY*, 1956 (UNIVERSAL).

June Cunningham

June Cunningham was one of the few British starlets who actually got to play a leading part (in the 1959 horror movie *Horrors of the Black Museum*) after playing supporting roles in two good movies. She was funny as the usherette in *The Smallest Show on Earth* (1957), and showed a sense of drama for her performance in *The Scamp* (1957). She was born as June Margaret Cunningham in 1935, in London, and started modeling at the age of 18. As June de Milo, she was photographed by Harrison Marks (who married his muse, blonde nude model Pamela Green, of *Peeping Tom* and *Naked as Nature Intended* fame). Only 20 years old, she married a guy named Monty Freedman and enrolled in acting classes at Aida Foster's. Her professional debut was made on British television in the first soap opera for adults, *The Grove Family*. June was seen on the show in the 1956-1957 season. (The series ran on the BBC from 1954-1957.) She appeared as a panel member on television in the popular *Yakity-Yak* show the next year, and played Rita Marlowe on stage in "Will Success Spoil Rock Hunter?" with Paul Carpenter. The show opened on August 25th, running for just six nights. When asked at the time what her plans for the future were, she answered: "My ambition is films. Dumb-blonde parts, of course; nice, unsophisticated and curvy." Well, that was actually all she got in the early sixties; dumb blonde roles in some minor comedies. (Including rival blonde Carole Lesley's *Three on a Spree*, 1961.) In 1963, she married actor Michael Standing and gave birth to their son, Seth. She focussed on married life and never returned to show business again.

JUNE CUNNINGHAM FILMOGRAPHY

1957: *The Smallest Show on Earth* (Marlene Hogg), *The Scamp* (Annette).
1959: *Horrors of the Black Museum* (Joan Berkeley).
1961: *Three on a Spree* (Rosie), *Part-Time Wife* (blonde).
1962: *Design for Loving* (Alice).
1963: *The Small World of Sammy Lee* (Rita).

WITH BILL TRAVERS IN *THE SMALLEST SHOW ON EARTH*, 1957 (BRITISH LION).

WITH TERENCE MORGAN, RICHARD ATTENBOROUGH AND COLIN PETERSEN IN
THE SCAMP, 1957.

GIRLS ON THE LOOSE, 1958 (UNIVERSAL).

Abby Dalton

Maybe this green-eyed blonde became most famous due to her television work in *Hennesey* in the sixties and *Falcon Crest* in the eighties, but in the fifties she starred in some Roger Corman movies and posed for some sexy layouts in then-hot men magazines. Abby Dalton was born Marlene Wasden, on August 15, 1935, in Las Vegas, Nevada. "My career started with dancing. But it was not a big success. I was always put in the front, because of my long legs. But after the first appearance I was put in the back row, because I was no prima ballerina!" Giving up on dancing, she tried modeling. That got her plenty of work and brought her to the attention of producer/director Roger Corman. Together with actresses like June Kenney, Dorothy Provine and Yvonne Lime, she dominated the juvenile delinquent/hot rod/girl gang movies that were really

WITH JAMES BEST IN *COLE YOUNGER, GUNFIGHTER*, 1958 (ALLIED ARTISTS).

ROCK ALL NIGHT, 1957 (AIP).

WITH BETSY JONES MORELAND IN *THE VIKING WOMEN AND THE SEA SERPENT*, 1957 (AIP).

popular with fifties teenagers. Her best parts were in non-Corman movies. For Warner Bros., she played in *Stakeout on Dope Street*, and Universal cast her in *Girls on the Loose* (both 1958). After those B-movies, Abby turned to television in the early sixties. That's where she reached real fame with the public, especially with her role of Nurse Martha Hale in the hit series *Hennesey* (1959-1962). After this series, she married businessman Jack Smith, and divided her time between her husband, two sons and a daughter and her career in television films and shows.

WITH JONATHAN HAZE IN *STAKEOUT ON DOPE STREET*, 1958 (WARNER BROS.)

ABBY DALTON FILMOGRAPHY

1957: *Carnival Rock, Teenage Doll, Rock All Night* (Julie), *The Viking Women and the Sea Serpent* (Desir).
1958: *Cole Younger, Gunfighter* (Lucy Antrim), *Stakeout on Dope Street* (Kathy), *Girls on the Loose* (Agnes Clark), *The High Cost of Loving* (Cora, a secretary).
1966: *The Plainsman* (Calamity Jane).
1976: *A Whale of a Tale* (Anne Fields).
1989: *Roller Blade Warriors: Taken by Force* (mother Speed).
1994: *CyberTracker* (Chief Olson).
1999: *Buck and the Magic Bracelet* (Ma Dalton).
2008: *Prank* (Mrs. Sweeney).

Vera Day

Born in London, on August 4, 1935, this petite British starlet was a hairdresser's model before getting on stage in *Wish You Were Here* and *Pal Joey* (both 1952). She then married body builder and would-be actor Arthur Mason, who also became her manager. (Although Vera Day married her muscleman three years earlier (in 1954), it still forced the press to compare them to US blonde Jayne Mansfield and former Mister Universe Mickey Hargitay later in her career.) In 1955 she got a part in Sir Carol Reed's classic *A Kid for Two Farthings*. This role was the stepping-stone for another important movie two years later. In *A Kid for Two Farthings*, Vera played dizzy blonde Mimi. She has a crush on Diana Dors' fiancé, Joe Robinson. The few speaking lines Miss Day has are funny and sharp. "Everybody seems to be going blonde around here. 'Marilyn Monroe,' it's come out like a sort of a rash," she tells Diana Dors when she visits her muscleman Joe in the gym where Vera works. Later on we see her dancing on the streets with real-life husband Arthur Mason. During the dance she only has eyes for Robinson who's waiting for Miss Dors. When Mason makes a comment about it, she answers: "You're for dancing, he's for looking." When she's gone over to Robinson, she flirts: "You know, sometimes I wish I was a bit more developed myself." These witty remarks became a kind of trademark for Vera during her career. She was often typecast as the sweet, but wisecracking dumb blonde. Producer Jack Hylton cast Vera as (surprise!) a sexy blonde in his 1955 Crazy Gang Revue, *Jokers Wild*. The image of Vera wearing a negligee with brief underwear was much publicized. When Sir Laurence Olivier was looking out for a young actress to portray Marilyn Monroe's showgirl colleague in *The Prince and the Showgirl* (1957), his search was over when he saw scenes of Vera from *A Kid for Two Farthings*. About her acting experience with Marilyn Monroe, Vera said in a *Picturegoer* interview: "Any disappointments I had were with the making of the film; the way I was pushed into a corner when Marilyn and I were in the same scene. And I had to wear a brown wig to cover my blonde hair — because, apologized Sir Laurence, 'you look so much like Marilyn.'" The Monroe movie gave Vera's film career a temporarily boost. She was cast for the part of the local barmaid in *Quatermass II* (1957). Vera was one of the victims of the mysterious toxic stones that fell from

the sky. A meatier role in *The Flesh is Weak* (1957), cast her as a prostitute. This movie was an American/British co-production starring John John Derek. *Picturegoer* magazine disliked the movie, but in its previews it mentioned Miss Day less harshly: "The film has a comely cast of fallen women — Vera Day, Shirley Ann Field, Patricia Jessel — any of whom would have shaped up better as the dull heroine than Milly Vitale." Another featured role was in the World War II

THE FLESH IS WEAK, 1957 (EROS).

drama, *I Was Monty's Double* (1958). She played the sexy secretary of John Mills. That same year she fell victim to murderer Boris Karloff in *Grip of the Strangler* (1958). Vera played a singer who is strangled and finished off with a blade in this chiller which was distributed as *The Haunted Strangler* in the USA. Her first starring role came with the horror movie *Womaneater* (1958), a low-budget thriller about a flesh-eating tree. She divorced Arthur Mason in 1958. In these days the British press romantically linked her to the former husband of Diana Dors, Dennis Hamilton. It was a short affair, because he died suddenly (presumably from a neglected venereal disease). She attended his funeral on February 4, 1959. In 1962 Vera auditioned for a part in the popular UK television series *The Avengers*. Out of 51 actresses, blonde Julie Stevens, Angela Douglas and Vera were selected. Miss Stevens eventually landed the role of nightclub singer Venus Smith. Vera Day starred in other moneymaking movies, but too many glamour poses may have proved her downfall in the early sixties. Her film career ended

WITH JOHN MILLS IN *I WAS MONTY'S DOUBLE*, 1958 (ABPC).

WITH DOROTHY SQUIRES AND NAT JACKLEY *IN STARS IN YOUR EYES*, 1956
(BRITISH LION).

WITH NORMAN WISDOM IN *A STITCH IN TIME*, 1963 (RANK).

WITH SHEILA O'NEILL AND JOSEPHINE ANNE IN CRAZY GANG REVUE 'JOKER'S WILD', 1955.

before she turned thirty! Vera Day married again, on November 28 1963, to photographer Terry O'Neill. (This marriage ended in divorce, too. In 1984 O'Neill would marry actress Faye Dunaway.) Out of movie work for some years, Vera Day was featured totally in the nude in a magazine called *On Location* in 1967. (The photos were shot by pin-up photographer Harrison Marks a while earlier and released in book form under the title *Vera*, around 1964.) In the late 1990s she surfaced again in *Lock, Stock and Two Smoking Barrels* (1998). She stayed blonde for all those years and, at age 64, still looked wonderful!

VERA DAY FILMOGRAPHY

1954: *Dance Little Lady* (babysitter), *The Crowded Day* (Suzy).
1955: *A Kid for Two Farthings* (Mimi).
1956: *It's a Great Day* (Blondie*)*, *Fun at St. Fanny's* (Maisie), *Stars in Your Eyes* (Maureen Temple).
1957: *The Prince and the Showgirl* (Betty), *Quatermass II* (Sheila), *Hell Drivers* (blonde), *The Flesh is Weak* (Edna).
1958: *Them Nice Americans* (Ann Adams), *Grip of the Strangler* (Pearl), *I Was Monty's Double* (Angela Cook), *A Clean Sweep* (Beryl Watson), *Womaneater* (Sally Norton), *Up the Creek* (Lily).
1959: *Too Many Crooks* (Charmaine).
1960: *And the Same to You* (Cynthia), *Trouble With Eve* (Daisy Freeman).
1961: *The Trunk* (Diane), *Watch it, Sailor!* (Shirley Hornett).
1963: *A Stitch in Time* (Betty), *Saturday Night Out* (Arlene).
1998: *Lock, Stock and Two Smoking Barrels* (Tanya).
2007: *The Riddle* (Sadie Miller).

Sandra Dorne

Husky-voiced, British platinum blonde actress Sandra Dorne started her career in the same year as her long-time friend Diana Dors. She was born Joanne Smith, on June 19, 1924, in Keighley, Yorkshire, England. Miss Dorne became a popular magazine pin-up and movie starlet in the late forties. She followed with acting lessons at the Rank Organisation's Charm School, but, because she felt she clashed with her pal Diana Dors, she asked for her release. Unlike Miss Dors, Sandra Dorne never reached major stardom and wasted the biggest part of her career in B-movies. In the forties she was mostly cast as good-time or wisecracking girls. The Hollywood-backed musical *Happy Go Lovely* (1951) had her cast as the colleague of showgirl Vera-Ellen. It was a dumb blonde role, and Sandra shared some nice scenes with Cesar Romero. In 1952 Sandra starred in a little thriller called *13 East Street*, opposite actor Patrick Holt. (Earlier in her career, she had a minor part in Holt's *Marry Me*, 1949.) Although there was 13 years of difference in age, they fell in love and got married in 1954. Together, they would also make *Alias John Preston*, *The Gelignite Gang* (both 1956) and *Operation Murder* (1957). 1953 proved to be a busy year, with six movies. Even though most of these parts were small, Sandra managed to leave her mark on the roles she played. She was unforgettable in director Peter Brooks' *The Beggar's Opera*, as the slatternly Sukey Tawdrey. In the female prison movie *The Weak and the Wicked* she had a small part alongside Diana Dors and Glynis Johns, but her role in *Marilyn* put her in the headlines. Sandra played the young wife

HAPPY GO LOVELY, 1951 (RKO).

WITH MAXWELL REED IN *MARILYN*, 1953.

of garage and pub owner Leslie Dwyer, who gets involved with Maxwell Reed, the new mechanic in her husband's garage. In the US the movie was released as *Roadhouse Girl*. In *The Yellow Balloon*, she is crook William Sylvester's accomplice who blackmails and finally tries to silence young Andrew Ray. That same year she had brothers Patric Doonan and Bryan Forbes fighting over her, when she played band singer Lucky Price in *Wheel of Fate*. Unlike Miss Dors, Sandra

POLICE DOG, 1955 (EROS).

lacked the gift of self-publicity. She didn't stand out enough between her contemporaries. Instead of accepting more film roles, Sandra concentrated on married life and was out of the movie business for over a year. (While researching her career it was remarkable to learn how minimal her entries in the then-popular British film magazines were.) She resumed her career acting in British B-movies. In *Final Column* (1955) Sandra plays the wife of a hypnotist who compels her to shoot her lover. He can't stop her, however, from also taking a fatal shot at him. In the late fifties Sandra was mostly seen on television and had the lead in a couple B-movies. In *The Bank Raiders* (1958), she plays a pretty crook who joins a gang of bank robbers, and in one of her final movies, *The House in Marsh Road* (1960), she was the wicked mistress of novelist Tony Wright. Together they plan the murder of his wife, but unfortunately things work out differently when a poltergeist stops them from pursuing their plan! In 1962 she played the part of showgirl Ruthine West in the television movie *Value for Money* (Diana Dors

WITH WAYNE MORRIS IN *THE GELIGNITE GANG*, 1956 (RENOWN PICTURES).

THE AMOROUS PRAWN, 1962 (BRITISH LION-COLUMBIA).

had played the same part in the 1955 movie version). Spending most of her time on television, Sandra did make the occasional film appearance during the fall of her show business career. In the author's opinion, Miss Dorne was an underrated actress; she always made the most of the material she was given. Sandra Dorne died in Westminster, London, on December 25, 1992. A year later, husband Patrick Holt also passed away.

SANDRA DORNE FILMOGRAPHY

1947: *Eyes That Kill* (Joan).

1948: *Once a Jolly Swagman* (Kay Fox), *Saraband for Dead Lovers, A Piece of Cake.*

1949: *Traveller's Joy* (Flower shop assistant), *Golden Arrow* (night club girl), *Marry Me, Helter Skelter* (Receptionist), *All Over the Town* (Marlene), *Don't Ever Leave Me* (Ruby Baines).

1950: *Don't Say Die* (Sandra), *The Miniver Story* (blonde in pub).

1951: *The Clouded Yellow* (Kyra), *Happy Go Lovely* (Betty Summers).

1952: *13 East Street* (Judy), *Hindle Wakes* (Mary Hollins).

1953: *Wheel of Fate* (Lucky Price), *Marilyn/Roadhouse Girl* (Marilyn Saunders), *The Weak and the Wicked* (Stella), *Alf's Baby* (Enid), *The Yellow Balloon* (Iris), *The Beggar's Opera* (Sukey Tawdrey).

1954: *The Good Die Young* (girl).

1955: *Police Dog* (blonde), *Final Column* (Anita Damon).

1956: *The Gelignite Gang/The Dynamiters* (Sally Morton), *Alias John Preston* (Sylvia/Maria), *The Iron Petticoat* (Tityana).

1957: *Three Sundays to Live* (Ruth Chapman), *Operation Murder* (Pat Wayne).

1958: *The Bank Raiders* (Della Byrne), *Orders to Kill* (blonde), *Portrait of a Matador.*

1960: *The Malpas Mystery* (Dora Elton), *The House in Marsh Road* (Valerie Stockley), *Not a Hope in Hell* (Diana Melton).

1962: *The Amorous Prawn* (Busty Babs).

1964: *Devil Doll* (Magda Gardinas), *The Secret Door* (Sonia).

1972: *All Coppers Are* (Sue's mother).

1977: *Joseph Andrews* (Whore in traffic jam).

1978: *The Playbirds* (secretary).

1987: *Eat the Rich* (Sandra).

Diana Dors

Diana Dors was called "Britain's first home grown sex symbol." In her heyday, sex on the British screen was mostly a matter of padded bras and low necklines. But real eroticism has little to do with skimpy-clad floozies or the amount of flesh exposed. She later commented on her screen persona, that her figure was fabulous, but her face had lips like rubber tires and eyes that were too small. Anyway, back in her starlet days, she carefully listened to her advisors to let the "blonde bombshell" tag get in the way of real ability as a character actress. Diana Mary Fluck was born October 23, 1931, in Swindon, England. Wanting to become a movie star all of her childhood and supported by her mother, Diana left for London at the age of 15. There she attended the Academy of Music and Dramatic Art and was given a spot in the film version of the West End thriller *The Shop at Sly Corner* (1947). After a couple of small movie parts, she caught the attention of Rank Studios' production head Sydney Box and was signed to a ten-year contract. In 1950, however, she was dropped, because they didn't know how to use her talents. She freelanced in a couple of B-movies, one of them being entitled *Lady Godiva Rides Again* (1951). In it she played a sharp-tongued beauty queen. Around this time she fell in love with playboy and women chaser Dennis Hamilton. Within the same year, on July 3 1951, they were married. Career wise, a nice role as a blackmailing shop assistant came with a thriller called *The Last Page* (1952). It started passé Hollywood actors George Brent and Marguerite Chapman, and was shown as *Man Bait* in the US cinemas. That same year she starred in West End flop, *Rendezvous*, with American dancer-comedian Walter Crisham. Diana had excellent notices in a play called *Remains to Be Seen* (December 1952), with Dickie Henderson. Her stage work brought Diana a lot of attention and a lot of offers. Laurence Olivier wanted her for a part in his upcoming film, *The Beggar's Opera* (1953), which he was casting. Diana declined Olivier (the role went to blonde actress/friend Sandra Dorne), but she took the offer of a summer season in Blackpool with the play *Life With the Lyons* (Blonde Belinda Lee would play Diana's part in the movie version the following year). More B-movies followed before she landed a role in an A-picture. Diana co-starred with Glynis Johns in the prison movie, *The Weak and the Wicked* (1953). By now the combination of hard work and her flair for

THE UNHOLY WIFE, 1957 (RKO).

making headlines, had made Diana a household name in Britain. She wasn't a real box-office hit, but she had an uncanny way of making headlines. In 1954 the British Parliament asked questions about her expenses. The publicity line on her was that she was Britain's Marilyn Monroe. Her hair had been platinum blonde for a couple of years now, and her pin-up poses were poor revamps of Monroe's. She was surely one of the most famous women in Britain and it was not surprising

WITH DAVID TOMLINSON AND PETER HAMMOND IN *VOTE FOR HUGGETT*, 1949 (GAINSBOROUGH PICTURES).

that she was offered a Rank contract again. She turned it down because director Sir Carol Reed wanted her for his *A Kid for Two Farthings* (1955). The critics were positive about Diana's role; they considered her the most convincing character in the movie. Fortified by her appearance in *A Kid for Two Farthings*, Diana told journalists, "I'm tired of always being the bad girl, the floozie, the sexy dame. I want to try to extend the range and try something a bit different…But not too different!" A starring role in the above-average B-comedy thriller *Miss Tulip Stays the Night* (1955), saw Diana in a unaccustomed role of the menaced heroine in a lonely house. Actress Cicely Courtneidge played the dual title role of a dizzy spinster and cold-blooded killer. Rank used her in a few comedies, but the roles *in As Long as They're Happy, Value for Money* and *An Alligator Named Daisy* (all 1955), mainly focussed on her sex appeal rather than her acting skills. *Picturegoer* raved about Diana's performance in *Value for Money*: "Diana Dors, extra blonde and extra glossy,

LADY GODIVA RIDES AGAIN, 1951 (BRITISH LION).

WITH ALAN SEDGWICK IN *MY WIFE'S LODGER*, 1952 (ADELPHI FILMS).

turns in a first-rate comedy performance," but found that "her ladylike role — in *An Alligator named* Daisy — [is] almost dull." She attended the Cannes Film Festival and was seen in a mink bikini in Italy, for the Venice Film Festival. 1956 marked the year of her big break. She starred as Mary Hilton in Lee Thompson's drama *Yield to the Night*. In this drama she played a good-time girl who kills the girlfriend of her lover Michael Craig, and is condemned to death by hanging.

THE SAINT'S RETURN, 1953 (HAMMER-RKO).

(Ruth Ellis was the real name of the lady who was the last woman to be sentenced to the death penalty a year earlier. Platinum blonde Miss Ellis once had a bit part in *Lady Godiva Rides Again* as one of the beauty contestants.) The critics were very enthusiastic about Diana's brilliant performance, and the movie received much international applause. Her role in *Yield to the Night* (released in the US by Allied Artists as *Blonde Sinner*) landed her a contract with Hollywood film studio RKO. In favor of RKO, Dennis Hamilton turned down a contract with 20th Century-Fox. They wanted her to star in *The Girl Can't Help It*. Of course, this part became a hit for newcomer Jayne Mansfield. On June 20, 1956, Diana boarded the *Queen Elizabeth* for her first RKO assignment, a comedy called *I Married a Woman*, with comedian George Gobel. While the Hamiltons were in the US, they also went to New York to catch the Broadway hit show *Will Success Spoil Rock Hunter?* Of its female star, Jayne Mansfield, Diana wrote in her weekly *Picturegoer* magazine column, *Out of Dors*: "People often accuse me of banging the publicity drum too

WITH PATRICK HOLT IN *MISS TULIP STAYS THE NIGHT*, 1955 (ADELPHI FILMS).

WITH JACK BUCHANAN IN *AS LONG AS THEY'RE HAPPY*, 1955 (RANK).

hard, but I'm a novice compared with Jayne." On her arrival in Hollywood, RKO held a press conference. There Diana was asked what she thought about her comparison to Marilyn Monroe. She answered, "If I must be compared to someone, it's not bad company!" Her second Hollywood film was a drama with Rod Steiger (with whom she had an affair during filming), called *The Unholy Wife* (1957). She played a B-girl who plots to murder her husband (Steiger) after falling in love

WITH VERA DAY AND LOU JACOBI IN A KID FOR TWO FARTHINGS, 1955 (LONDON FILM PRODUCTIONS).

with Tom Tryon. Looking back, it can be said that her choice of RKO wasn't a wise one. The studio system was falling apart and RKO would shut its doors in 1959. (Both movies Diana made at RKO were released by Universal Studios.) Both her Hollywood movies were box-office flops, and in November 1956 Diana returned home. She took a two-week break, vacationing with Dennis and actor friends Sandra Dorne and Patrick Holt in Malaga, before she started working on *The Long Haul* (1957), an American-backed film, as a blonde menace and homewrecker (Victor Mature's). It was here that she met and flirted with bit-part actor Tommy Yeardye, who was also functioning as Victor Mature's stand-in. Her return to the stage at the Coventry Theatre with the "Diana Dors Show" was a well publicized and well-timed event. Spectacularly gowned, supported by a bevy of young males in the best Mae West tradition, she sang and danced through several musical numbers. Her short Hollywood adventure had made her an international name; and in 1958 she left for Italy to play the lead in *La Ragazza del Palio*. She played

BELGIAN POSTER FOR *PASSPORT TO SHAME*, 1959 (BRITISH LION).

a Texas gas-station girl courted by impoverished prince Vittorio Gassmann who thinks she's an heiress. She also toured nightclubs and theatres all around Europe that year. Her marriage to Dennis Hamilton had become a farce by now. The couple lived separately since 1957 because Diana by now was romantically involved with former boxer Tommy Yeardye. On January 31 1959, Dennis Hamilton died quite suddenly. Within three months, Diana married comedian Dickie Dawson,

SCENT OF MYSTERY, 1960.

who appeared with her on television in *The Diana Dors Show*. The service was held in New York, where she appeared on *The Steve Allan Show* that same day! 1960 had her back in Hollywood for two guest appearances. One was with Danny Kaye in *On the Double* (1961) and the other was the gangster biopic *King of the Roaring Twenties* (1961), with Diana as a showgirl/moll. There were character roles in a couple of programmers, *Mrs. Gibbons' Boys* (1962) and *West 11* (1963), which saw the first of Diana's middle-aged character tarts, a lady with a kind heart but sleazy moral code. But she looked her old glamorous self in the French/British production *Allez France* (1964), a comedy about French football supporters in London, which was a success in France only. Stage work continued thereafter, mostly in Northern England, working men's clubs. Her marriage with Dawson ended in divorce in 1967. The couple had two sons who stayed to live with their father. The film roles she was offered were small: *Berserk* (1967), with Joan Crawford, *Danger Route* (1967) a spy thriller with Richard Johnson, and *Hammerhead* (1968), in which she was seen as an evil resort operator. On November 23, 1968, Diana married for the third time. Her marriage to actor Alan Lake was held at Caxton Hall, where she had married Dennis Hamilton all those years before. Their son Jason was born in 1969. In the seventies a stage part in *Three Months Gone* (1973), brought her excellent notices, and on television she had her own series called *Queenie's Castle*. She played the sharp-tongued and sexy-looking Yorkshire mother

WITH ERIC PORTMAN IN *WEST 11*, 1963 (ABPC).

Queenie Shepherd, in this hit show. Now frankly stout, but still posing for pin-ups, she played in a couple of soft-core sex comedies like *Bedtime with Rosie* (1975) and *Adventures of a Private Eye* (1977), to which her name was an asset. She began writing her life story and other saucy books during this period and appeared regularly on television talk shows. While filming her last movie, *Steaming* (1984), Diana found out she had cancer. She died on May 4, 1984.

DIANA DORS FILMOGRAPHY

1947: *The Shop at Sly Corner* (girl), *Dancing with Crime* (Annette), *Holiday Camp* (jitterbugger).
1948: *Good Time Girl* (Lyla Lawrence), *Penny and the Pownall* Case (Molly James), *The Calendar* (Hawkins), *My Sister and I* (dreary girl), *Oliver Twist* (Charlotte), *Here Come the Huggett's* (Diana Hopkins).

1949: *Vote for Huggett* (Diana), *It's Not Cricket* (blonde), *A Boy, a Girl and a Bike* (Ada Foster), *Diamond City* (Dora Bracken).

1950: *Dance Hall* (Carol).

1951: *Worm's Eye View* (Thelma), *Lady Godiva Rides Again* (Dolores August).

1952: *The Last Page/Man Bait* (Ruby Bruce), *My Wife's Lodger* (Eunice Higginbotham).

1953: *Is Your Honeymoon Really Necessary?* (Candy Markham), *The Saint's Return/The Saint's Girl Friday* (girl), *It's a Grand Life* (Cpl. Paula Clements), *The Weak and the Wicked* (Betty Brown).

1955: *Miss Tulip Stays the Night* (Kate Dax), *As Long As They're Happy* (Pearl), *A Kid for Two Farthings* (Sonia), *Value for Money* (Ruthine West), *An Alligator Named Daisy* (Vanessa Colebrook).

1956: *Yield to the Night/Blonde Sinner* (Mary Hilton), *I Married a Woman* (Janice Briggs).

1957: *The Unholy Wife* (Phyllis Hochen), *The Long Haul* (Lynn).

1958: *La Ragazza del Palio/The Love Specialist* (Diana Dixon), *Tread Softly Stranger* (Calico).

1959: *Passport to Shame* (Vicki).

1960: *Scent of Mystery* (Winifred Jordan).

1961: *On the Double* (Sgt. Bridget Stanhope), *King of the Roaring Twenties* (Madge).

1962: *Mrs. Gibbons' Boys* (Myra).

1963: *West 11* (Georgia).

1964: *Allez France* (herself).

1966: *The Sandwich Man* (Billingsgate woman).

1967: *The Plank* (woman in window), *Berserk* (Matilda), *Danger Route* (Rhoda Gooderich).

1968: *Hammerhead* (Kit), *Baby Love* (Liz).

1970: *There's a Girl in My Soup* (wife), *Deep End* (lady client).

1971: *Hannie Caulder* (Madame), *The Pied Piper* (Frau Poppendick).

1972: *The Amazing Mr. Blunden* (Mrs. Wickens).

1973: *Nothing But the Night* (Anna Harb), *Theatre of Blood* (Mrs. Psaltery), *Steptoe and Son Ride Again* (woman).

1974: *From Beyond the Grave* (Mabel Lowe), *Craze* (Dolly Newman).

1975: *The Amorous Milkman* (Rita Jones), *Swedish Wildcats, Bedtime with Rosie* (Annie), *Three for All* (Mrs. Ball).

1976: *Keep it Up Downstairs* (Daisy Dureneck), *Adventures of a Taxi Driver* (Mrs. North).

1977: *Adventures of a Private Eye* (Mrs. Horne).

1979: *Confessions from the David Galaxy Affair* (Jennie Stride).

1985: *Steaming* (Violet).

Anita Ekberg

This blue-eyed, statuesque actress once was Miss Sweden. She had a Hollywood career in B-movies, before she landed the role which made her famous all around the world, in Federico Fellini's *La Dolce Vita* (1959). She was born, the sixth of eight children, as Kerstin Anita Marianne Ekberg, on September 29, 1931, in Malmö, Sweden. Anita grew up with six brothers and one sister. Her father worked as a foreman for a company which supplied coal to ships in Malmö harbour. Said to be a shy child, she had few playmates beside her sister Inga and brother Goran. At school Anita was a poor student in everything except cooking and sewing. When she finished school at sixteen, she found work in a department store. Her pretty face and slim figure brought her to the attention of the manager of the women's dresses department, and soon she began to model clothes. Enthusiastic about modeling, Anita entered the "Miss Hipp" contest at the Hippodrome Theatre. When she won first prize, she was offered a trip to Hollywood. Because her parents found her too young, they refused to let her leave the country. But at the age of twenty she became Miss Sweden and visited the United States to compete for the Miss Universe title. She didn't win, but together with some other contestants she was signed by Universal-International. She spent many months studying drama, diction, etc. at the studio, before she was used as decorative background in a few of their productions. In 1952 she was introduced by glamour photographer Bruno Bernard to actor-director Hugo Haas, who was searching for a new blonde to star in his seedy melodramas. Haas declined Anita thinking she was too sexy. (He later "settled" for Cleo Moore.) When Marilyn Monroe wasn't available, Bob Hope asked the unknown Anita to join him visiting the troops in Alaska for one of his U.S.O. tours. She was a sensation with the soldiers, and their reaction was heard all the way back in Hollywood. The U.S.O. tour didn't get her a contract right away, but it did get her a lot of attention. A year later she screen tested for the television series, *Sheena, Queen of the Jungle*. The producers wanted her for the part, but Anita backed off because she was offered a movie role beside John Wayne and Lauren Bacall, *Blood Alley* (1955). It was a non-glamorous role; as Wei Ling, Anita was almost unrecognizable in her black wig. Due to her many pin-up poses, she received more publicity than any other star in Hollywood. At

the time she told *Show* magazine: "I try to look plain, but nothing looks plain on me. I just can't hide my figure." At Paramount she played herself in movies like *Artists and Models* (1955) and *Hollywood or Bust* (1956). When actress Arlene Dahl wasn't available for *War and Peace* (1956), Anita stepped in and got her first important film part. Since her other roles at Paramount were mere decorative ones, the press had high hopes that Anita would prove she could act. And

DAS LIEBESKARUSELL, 1965 (INTERCONTINENTAL FILM).

although it was a small role, the critics were positive about her acting skills. On February 23, 1956, Anita won the Golden Globe award for "Most Promising Female Newcomer." Then Anita got a two-picture deal at RKO. The little crime movie *Man in the Vault* (1956) again gave her a good chance to display her qualities in acting. In *Back from Eternity* (1956), she was seen as a B-girl who survives a plane crash. It was the meatiest role, acting wise, she had so far. Then Columbia, which already had Kim Novak as their blonde glamour queen, used her for *Zarak* (1956). In it she plays an Indian dancer and love interest of Victor Mature, and is seen in some very skimpy outfits and sexy dance numbers. *Picturegoer* wrote the following review about the movie: "This must be seen to be believed. Everyone involved in it should get an Oscar for absurdity." There wasn't much applause for Anita's part either: "The slinky blonde native in a bit of gauze held up by sequins is Anita Ekberg, who does a dance in which she lies on the floor and wriggles." While in England to film *Interpol* (1957), she was introduced to Queen Elizabeth II. During this Royal Command Performance, she met British beefcake actor Anthony Steel. They fell in love and married on May 22, 1956, in Florence,

ZARAK, 1956 (COLUMBIA).

Italy. The next year they made a movie together. The western/drama *Valerie* (1957) received bad comments. *Picturegoer* magazine wrote: "If this doesn't explode the myth that maybe there's an actress luring behind the Ekberg shape, nothing can." In 1958 Anita filed for divorce, because she could stand Steel's jealousy. (In 1956 Anita posed nude for sculptor Sepy Dobronyi. During her marriage some of his photos showed up in *Playboy* magazine, making Steel very angry.) The couple sep-

INTERPOL, 1957 (COLUMBIA).

arated in January 1959 and were granted a divorce on May 14, 1959. That same year she left for Italy to make *Nel Segno di Roma*, with Georges Marchal. After seeing her in this movie, director Fellini asked her to play an American movie star visiting Rome in his next film. Together with Marcello Mastroianni she shared the most famous scene in *La Dolce Vita* (1959): shot in the middle of the winter, Anita wades through the Roman Trevi fountains; a scene which became immortal in cinema history. Anita stayed in Italy and made a couple successful movies there. She played a serious role as a missionary in *Apocalisse sul Fiume Giallo* (1960), with Georges Marchal. And, beside Daniel Gélin and Vittorio de Sica, she was a Spanish town tramp who must use her charms to soothe an occupying colonel in *Les trois etcetera du Colonel* (1960). The next year she played the cruel mistress of Mongol warlord Genghis Khan (played by Jack Palance) in *I Mongoli* (1961). Anita had a sexy part in *Boccaccio '70* (1962). The film had four separate segments directed by different directors. Fellini directed Anita again in the episode *Le tentazioni del dottor Antonio*, as a girl in a roadside billboard who comes to life and seduces Dr. Antonio (Peppino De Filippo). In 1963 she returned to Hollywood

BACK FROM ETERNITY, 1956 (RKO).

WITH MYRNA HANSEN, KATHLEEN HUGHES AND PIPER LAURIE IN *THE GOLDEN BLADE*, 1953 (UNIVERSAL).

to star besides her friends Bob Hope and Frank Sinatra, in *Call Me Bwana and Four for Texas* respectively. She married actor Rick Van Nutter on April 9 that same year in Switzerland. Together they had one child. (Anita had two miscarriages before this child was born.) Old friend Jerry Lewis asked her to take part in what would become his worst comedy, *Way… Way Out* (1966). Acting mostly in European movies throughout the late sixties and seventies, she posed nude

WITH MARCELLO MASTROIANNI IN *LA DOLCE VITA*, 1959 (GLORIA FILMS).

(slightly overweight) in 1978. Earlier, in 1970, she divorced Van Nutter, having lived separately for a couple of years already. Besides her nude layouts in European magazines, she hit the low point in her career with a nightclub act in Munich's Moulin Rouge nightclub. Besides playing the occasional brothel madam, Anita seemed almost forgotten by film producers, but in 1987 she made her comeback on the big screen. Fellini asked her to star in his film *Intervista*, together with Marcello Mastroianni again. The scenes where he visits Miss Ekberg are magical. Still making the occasional movie appearance, Anita has lived as a single woman in Italy since 1975 and is one of the last surviving fifties movie blondes.

ANONIMA COCOTTES, 1960 (COCINOR).

ANITA EKBERG FILMOGRAPHY

1953: *The Mississippi Gambler* (bridesmaid), *Take Me to Town* (dancehall girl), *Abbott and Costello Go to Mars* (Venusian Guard), *The Golden Blade* (handmaiden).

1955: *Blood Alley* (Wei Ling), *Artists and Models* (Anita).

1956: *War and Peace* (Helene), *Hollywood or Bust* (Anita), *Man in the Vault* (Flo Randall), *Back from Eternity* (Rena), *Zarak* (Salma).

1957: *Interpol/Pickup Alley* (Gina Broger), *Valerie* (Valerie).

1958: *Paris Holiday* (Zara), *Screaming Mimi* (Virginia Wilson), *The Man Inside* (Trudie Hall).

1959: *Nel Segno di Roma* (Queen Zenobia), *La Dolce Vita* (Sylvia).

1960: *Apocalisse sul Fiume Giallo* (Dorothy Simmons), *Les Trois etcetera du Colonel* (Georgina), *Anonima Cocottes*.

1961: *I Mongoli* (Hulina), *A Porte Chiuse* (Olga Duvovich).

1962: *Boccaccio '70* (Anita), *Lykke og Krone* (herself).

1963: *Call Me Bwana* (Luba), *Four for Texas* (Elya Carlson).

1964: *Bianco, Rosso, Giallo, Rosa* (Alberchiaria).

1965: *Das Liebeskarusell* (Lolita Young), *The Alphabet Murders* (Amanda Beatrice Cross).

1966: *Way...Way Out* (Anna Soblova), *Das Gewisse Etwas der Frauen* (Margaret Joyce).

1967: *Il Cobra* (Lou), *Woman Times Seven* (Claudie), *La Sfinge d'Oro* (Paulette), *Scusi, lei è favorevole o contrario ?* (Baroness Olga).

1968: *Crónica de un Atraco* (Bessie).

1969: *If It's Tuesday, This Must be Belgium* (performer), *Malenka* (Malenka), *Un Sudario a la Medida* (Jacqueline), *Blonde Köder für den Mörder* (Mrs. Ferretti).

1970: *Quella Chiara Notte d'Ottobre, Il Divorzio* (Flavia), *Il Debito Coniugale.*

1971: *I Clowns* (herself).

1972: *North-East of Seoul, La Lunga Cavalcata della Vendetta.*

1973: *Casa d'Appuntamento* (Madamme Colette).

1975: *El Valle de las Viudas.*

1978: *Suor Omicidi/The Killer Nun* (Sister Gertrude).

1979: *Gold of the Amazon Women* (Queen Na-Eela).

1980: *S.H.E.* (Dr. Else Biebling).

1982: *Cicciabomba.*

1987: *Intervista* (herself), *Dolce Pelle di Angela* (Signora Rocchi).

1991: *Il Conte Max* (Marika).

1992: *Cattive Ragazze, Ambrogio* (Clarice).

1996: *Bámbola* (Mamma Greta), *La Signora della Città.*

1998: *Le Nain Rouge* (Paola Bendoni).

LOBBY CARD FOR *SCREAMING MIMI*, 1958 (COLUMBIA).

OUTLAW WOMEN, 1952 (LIPPERT).

Dolores Fuller

Cult director Edward Wood's muse Dolores Fuller only played leading roles in the grade-Z movies he produced and directed. The rest of her movie career she had small parts in high-grade Hollywood productions and bit parts in a couple of B-movies. Dolores Eble was born in 1923, in South Bend, Indiana. It all started at the early age of 10, when she had a cameo part in the motel scene of *It Happened One Night* (1934), with Clark Gable. As a teenager Dolores acted in school plays and was a model before she got small parts in movies and on television. A divorced mother of two, she entered a mother-daughter beauty contest in July 1951. She and her daughter Connie Rae came in second. Hollywood called, and Dolores made her adult debut in the western *Outlaw Women* (1952), with Marie Windsor and Alan Nixon. Of course, she's best remembered

WITH ED WOOD IN *GLEN OR GLENDA*, 1953 (SCREEN CLASSICS).

today for her romance with Edward Wood and the part she played in his *Glen or Glenda* (1953). "I was a young girl when I met Edward D. Wood at an interview. He told me, right then and there, he was going to make me a star. He planned to star me in several of his films. Of course, I probably didn't believe him. But it

BODY BEAUTIFUL, 1953 (ROADSHOW PICTURES).

sounded nice and I went along with it." Her next part for Wood was in *Jail Bait* (1954), maybe the best of Wood's directing efforts. Nevertheless, after *Jail Bait*, Dolores' career sagged. She lost the leading part in Wood's *Bride of the Monster* (1955), because Wood replaced her with Loretta King, whose millionaire father was supposed to finance his project. After living together a few years, Dolores left Wood when his drinking problem got worse. She was Dinah Shore's double on *The Dinah Shore Chevy Show* (1956). She quit the movie business in 1956 and became a songwriter. Her ability as a songwriter manifested itself through the intervention of her friend, producer Hal Wallis. Dolores had wanted to get an acting role in the Elvis Presley movie *Blue Hawaii* (1961), which Wallis was producing, but instead he put her in touch with Hill & Range, the publisher that provided Presley with songs. Fuller went into a collaborative partnership with composer Ben Weisman and got one song, "Rock-A-Hula Baby," into the movie. It was a beginning of what eventually led to Elvis Presley recording a dozen of her songs, including "I Got Lucky" and "Spinout." She wrote songs for nine of Elvis Presley's movies (in the period 1961-1969). On August 8, 1988, she married her second husband, Philip Chamberlin. In the late nineties (after Sarah Jessica Parker portrayed her in Tim Burton's *Ed Wood*, 1994), she played some small parts in a couple of B-horror movies. Well in her eighties, Dolores Fuller resides in Las Vegas, Nevada.

WITH CLANCY MALONE IN *JAIL BAIT*, 1954 (HOWCO).

DOLORES FULLER FILMOGRAPHY

1934: *It Happened One Night* (child).
1952: *Outlaw Women* (saloon girl).
1953: *Body Beautiful* (June, a model), *Girls in the Night* (beauty contestant), *The Blue Gardenia* (woman at bar), *Count the Hours* (reporter), *The Moonlighter*, *Mesa of Lost Women* (watcher in the woods), *Glen or Glenda* (Barbara).
1954: *College Capers*, *The Raid*, *Playgirl* (girl), *This is My Love*, *Jail Bait* (Marilyn Gregor).
1955: *Bride of the Monster* (Margie).
1956: *The Opposite Sex*.
1997: *The Ironbound Vampire* (Theresa Powell).
1998: *Dimensions in Fear* (TV station owner).
2001: *The Corpse Grinders 2* (Patricia Grant).

LUST TO KILL, 1957 (PRODUCTION ASSOCIATES).

Sandra Giles

Movie starlet Sandra Giles was born Leila Bernice Giles, on July 24, 1932, in Hooker, Oklahoma. She was raised in Texas and when she was twelve she was put in foster care in San Antonio. Sandra's father had gone to jail for molesting her and her mother waited tables all night and slept all day. After Bernice and her sister were sent to foster homes, she just took off. A few years later, when her mother, now divorced, moved to Anaheim, Bernice hitchhiked across the country to be with her. Sandra won several beauty titles, before she moved to Hollywood in 1953. In Hollywood she started working as a secretary and book-keeper in a Jewish delicatessen. In 1956 she tried modeling, and it was roommate Juli Reding who suggested taking up a contact with her agent Sheldon Davis. Sandra got quite some publicity when she revealed a painting of herself as "Lady Luck" at the Fremont Hotel in Las Vegas. When the painting was revealed, Sandra was shocked, because she was painted in the nude. Later, Sandra would declare to several journalists that she had posed in a bathing suit. She sued both the artist, Philip Paval, and the hotel. The case was settled out of court, leaving Sandra with $15,000. In an interview, she called the settlement "satisfactory." It paid the costs of getting started in show business: "You need a car and some good clothes. And I'm spending eighty dollars a week on drama and diction and singing lessons. I make as much as I did as a secretary. Of course you have to spend twice as much; on clothes and hairdos." In 1957 she was a Boom-Boom girl on the Tom Duggan television show and starred in the TV pilot *Richard Diamond, Private Detective*" with David Janssen. She was said to be having an affair with him at this time. In the cinemas she was seen as a saloon girl in a Western called *Lust to Kill* (1957) and British *Picturegoer* magazine described her as "a mixture of the best of Jayne Mansfield with the best of Mamie Van Doren." With these two blondes and fellow starlets Juli Reding and Kathy Mar-lowe she appeared with master of ceremony Tommy Noonan at the Hollywood Ballyhoo Ball of 1958. When the latter got her moment of fame to star in the cheaply-made *Girl with an Itch* (1958), Sandra landed herself a small part in that movie, too. She got herself some publicity being chosen "Miss Press Club," and arriving in a mink-covered car at the premiere of *Teacher's Pet* (1958) led

to a three-page article about her in *Life* magazine. A screen test for *God's Little Acre* (1958) was lost to Fay Spain, but being the girlfriend of producer Elmer Rhoden secured her a starring role in the low-budget movie *Daddy-O* (1959). In this teenage/road movie Sandra played the "hard to get" new girl in town

WITH DICK CONTINO IN *DADDY-O*, 1959 (AIP).

who falls for truck driver/singer Dick Contino. The movie was a flop commercially and after a cameo appearance (as a brunette) in the Shirley MacLaine/David Niven comedy, *Ask Any Girl* (1959), Sandra quit filmmaking for a while. In December 1960, she married for the second time. Her husband is wealthy Orange County builder Paul Robertson. During the sixties Sandra appeared in the theatre (e.g., in *The Odd Couple*, 1967, with Tony Randall, Mickey Rooney and Vikki Dougan) and made a couple of movies, all as a brunette. In March 1966 she divorced Robertson. A nice, but small, part came her way in *Flareup* (1969) as a colleague of go-go dancer Raquel Welch. Nowadays, Sandra is back to being blonde and owns a restaurant called "Passion" in California.

1957: *Lust to Kill* (Belle).

1958: *Girl with an Itch* (girl), *The Matchmaker* (blonde), *Lost, Lonely and Vicious* (Darlene).

1959: *Daddy-O* (Jana Ryan), *Ask Any Girl* (redhead).

1963: *McLintock!* (saloon girl), *It Happened at the World's Fair* (June).

1965: *Black Spurs* (Sadie's girl).

1967: *Border Lust*.

1969: *Flareup* (Nikki).

1972: *Black Gunn* (prostitute), *Last of the Red Hot Lovers*.

1973: *The Mad Bomber* (checkout girl).

1978: *Are You in the House Alone?* (Hostess).

1981: *A Ticket to Heaven* (airport bookseller), *Crazy Times* (Esther).

LOBBY CARD FOR *LOST, LONELY AND VICIOUS*, 1958 (HOWCO).

Ingrid Goude

Swedish Ingrid Goude was brought to America for the Miss Universe contest of 1956. She came all the way from Sandviken, Sweden (where she was born in 1937), to Los Angeles to make a few movies under contract at Universal. She had won the Swedish beauty pageant and became second runner-up in the Miss Universe contest. (Winner Carol Morris and 1st runner-up Marina Orschel were also offered contracts by Universal.) After a few small parts and a role on television in *The Bob Cummings Show* (1957-1958), she asked for and was granted her release from her studio agreement in January 1958. Her first (and last) freelance movie was a low-budget horror movie called *The Killer Shrews* (1959). This movie received cult status in later days and

marked Ingrid's only starring role. After a part in an episode (called "Charity Affair") of *Richard Diamond, Private Detective* (1959) and a recurring role in *Steve Canyon* (1959-60) on television, she ended her showbiz career. Ingrid Goude married Jerome Ohrbach, president of Ohrbach's department stores, in April 1962. Ingrid Goude never reached the same level of stardom as the other Miss Sweden contestant, Anita Ekberg.

INGRID GOUDE FILMOGRAPHY

1957: *The Tattered Dress* (girl by pool).
1958: *The Big Beat* (secretary), *Wild Heritage* (Hilda Jansen), *Once Upon a Horse* (Beulah, bride), *Never Steal Anything Small* (model).
1959: *Holiday for Lovers* (receptionist), *The Killer Shrews* (Ann Craigis).

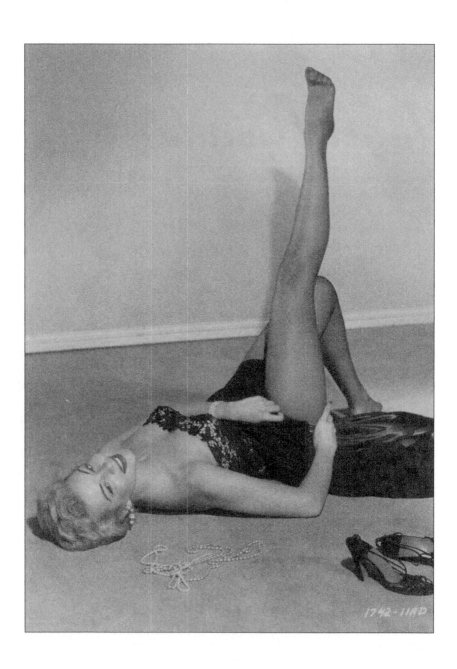

Kathleen Hughes

Elizabeth Margaret van Gerkan was born on November 14, 1928, in Holly-wood. She was under contract to 20th Century-Fox from 1948 'til 1951. When they dropped her she freelanced for a year. In 1952 she made *For Men Only* with Paul Henreid and her agent landed her a seven-year contract with Univer-sal. There she played different parts in Westerns, science-fiction and adventure movies. *It Came from Outer Space* (Universal's first entry into the 3-D medium) and *The Glass Web* (both 1953) are two movies that have reached some kind of cult status these days. The latter tells the story of the greedy blonde bit player Paula (Hughes), who has a romance with a TV scriptwriter (John Forsythe), but is also flirting with the casting director (Edward G. Robinson). At one point she decides to blackmail the writer, then gets in a fight with the casting direc-tor and receives a threatening call from her ex-husband. Later that same day she's found dead. English *Picturegoer* magazine wrote about Kathleen's perform-ance: "Kathleen Hughes brings a lively flamboyance to the brief, but telling, role of the conniving victim." Kathleen Hughes was released from her contract on May 27, 1954. After her release, she auditioned for and landed the lead in the off-Broadway stage version of *The Seven Year Itch*. (Vanessa Brown had played the role on Broadway and, of course, Marilyn Monroe played "the girl upstairs" in the film version.) On July 25, 1954, Kathleen married Universal producer Stanley Rubin. After the birth of her first son (two sons and a daughter would follow) she stopped acting for a while. In 1956 she starred in a B-movie called *Three Bad Sisters*, with Sara Shane and Marla English. Kathleen Hughes played the meanest of the three Craig sisters. United Artists publicized Kathleen's part as follows: "Kathleen Hughes plays a sadistic young woman with a lust to kill, completely without morals!" Besides being known as a "bad girl," Kathleen was named "The 3-D Girl" by the Manhattan Film Projectionists' Union, with "3-D" standing for "devastating, delightful and delicious." Nevertheless, she didn't get a starring role in a movie the remainder of her career. She did play in a lot of television shows like *The Bob Cummings Show* (1958), *Hotel de Paree* (1959) and *Bachelor Father* (1962). 80-year-old Kathleen Hughes is a beloved guest at sci-ence-fiction movie conventions these days.

THE GOLDEN BLADE, 1953 (UNIVERSAL).

WITH ANN BLYTH AND HUGH O'BRIAN IN *SALLY AND SAINT ANNE*, 1952
(UNIVERSAL).

WITH EDWARD G. ROBINSON IN *THE GLASS WEB*, 1953 (UNIVERSAL).

WITH RORY CALHOUN IN *DAWN AT SOCORRO*, 1954 (UNIVERSAL).

KATHLEEN HUGHES FILMOGRAPHY

1949: *Mother is a Freshman* (Rhoda Adams), *Mr. Belvedere Goes to College* (Kay Nelson), *It Happens Every Spring* (Sarah).

1950: *Where the Sidewalk Ends* (secretary), *Mister 880* (secretary), *I'll Get By* (secretary).

1951: *Take Care of My Little Girl* (Jenny Barker), *I'll See you in My Dreams* (nurse).

1952: *For Men Only/The Tall Lie* (Tracy Norman), *Sally and Saint Anne* (Lois Foran).

1953: *Thy Neighbor's Wife, The Golden Blade* (Bakhamra), *It Came from Outer Space* (Jane), *The Glass Web* (Paula Rainier).

1954: *Dawn at Socorro* (Clare).

1955: *Cult of the Cobra* (Julia Thompson).

1956: *Three Bad Sisters* (Valerie Craig).

1958: *Unwed Mother* (Linda).

1967: *The President's Analyst* (White House tourist).

1975: *Babe* (Nancy Armitage).

1977: *The Spell* (Fenetia).

1979: *And Your Name is Jonah* (Nurse Hubert).

1990: *Revenge* (Mother Superior).

Martha Hyer

Martha Hyer was born on August 10, 1924, in Fort Worth, Texas. During her high school days she was very ambitious about becoming a movie star. After graduation she joined the Pasadena Playhouse in California to study drama. An agent saw her in a play and Martha was invited to Hollywood to read at Paramount. But nothing came of it. A year later her agent arranged an interview at RKO studios. RKO signed her and she appeared in their routine programmers. When Howard Hughes took over RKO in 1949, her option was dropped. "It was another bad period in the industry. Production was off again and jobs were anything but plentiful. I did several films freelance — one in Australia [*The Kangaroo Kid*, 1950]. And after that, I did a couple of small ones. And then I got married." Martha married writer/director Ray Stahl in 1951. The couple lived in Japan for almost a year

WITH DAVID NIVEN IN *MY MAN GODFREY*, 1957 (UNIVERSAL).

For Bob —
With my very best wishes —
Good Luck!
Martha Hyer

and Martha made two pictures there. Husband Stahl directed her in *Geisha Girl* and *Oriental Evil* (both 1951). Then she moved to London for three months and then to Africa, where they lived for six months and worked on a British picture together. After the completion of their movie, *The Scarlet Spear* (1954), the couple decided to separate and Martha returned to Hollywood in 1953. Luckily for her, she was almost immediately booked for a role in Warner Bros.' *So Big* (1953). "I

WITH VAN JOHNSON IN *WIVES AND LOVERS*, 1963 (PARAMOUNT).

was delighted with this part, because it meant I could play 'the other woman'— so different from the many ingénue roles I'd had in the past. I really welcomed the change." Having been a brunette all this time, her role in *So Big* needed her to be reddish-brown. Then came a part with Doris Day in *Lucky Me* (1954). Because there couldn't be two blondes in the picture, she became a redhead. And when she teamed up with brunette Audrey Hepburn for *Sabrina* (1954), she became a blonde. In 1955 she was under contract to Universal studios. They wanted her to become a brunette again, but two years later she changed her hair color to blonde definitely. This also made a change in the parts she was offered. Usually cast as the nice girl, she now landed roles as the spoilt, sophisticated blonde and she was named "Universal's answer to Grace Kelly." "It was a long battle. Every time I asked for a 'bad' role, studio executives told me: 'Nice girls, convincing ones, are hard to find. Stay that way.' But I won!" At Universal she was kept busy in Westerns, dramas and comedies, and Miss Hyer proved herself a versatile actress. In many movies she played "the other woman." In Universal's *Mister Cory* (1957), she plays the snobbish sister of Kathryn Grant. At first Mr. Cory (Tony Curtis) falls for her, but after

WITH VAN JOHNSON IN *KELLY AND ME*, 1957 (UNIVERSAL).

WITH WILLIAM REYNOLDS AND TONY CURTIS IN *MISTER CORY*, 1957 (UNIVERSAL).

WITH FRANKIE VAUGHAN IN *THE RIGHT APPROACH*, 1961 (20TH CENTURY FOX).

learning her true nature, he chooses her sister. In Paramount's *Houseboat* (1958) she lost Cary Grant to Sophia Loren. In United Artists' *Paris Holiday* (1958), it is voluptuous Anita Ekberg who steals Bob Hope away from Martha. And after dating Frank Sinatra in MGM's *Some Came Running* (1958), he still can't get Shirley MacLaine out of his head. Her role of schoolteacher Gwen French in the latter got her nominated for the Academy Award as Best Supporting Actress in 1958. She lost to Wendy Hiller (for her role in *Separate Tables*). After a trip to Germany in 1959, she was in the running for the role of Marion Crane in Hitchcock's *Psycho* (1960), but lost out to Janet Leigh. In the sixties, Martha played some sexy parts. She was at her "trashy" best in *The Carpetbaggers* (1964) as a hooker. And that same year she was the disturbed mistress of Barry Sullivan in *Fuego*. When Sullivan wants to end the affair to go back to his wife and daughter, Martha gets revenge on him and burns down his house. The movie was filmed in Spain and released in the United States by American-International Pictures as *Pyro*. Her second marriage was to Paramount producer Hal Wallis from 1966 until his death in 1986. Martha's autobiography, *Finding My Way*, was published in 1990.

MARTHA HYER FILMOGRAPHY

1946: *The Locket* (bridesmaid).
1947: *Thunder Mountain* (Ellie Jorth), *Born to Kill* (maid), *Woman on the Beach* (Mrs. Barton).
1948: *The Velvet Touch* (Helen Adams), *Gun Smugglers* (Judy Davis), *The Judge Steps Out* (Catherine Bailey).
1949: *Clay Pigeon* (Miss Harwick), *Roughshod* (Marcia), *Rustlers* (Ruth Abbott).
1950: *The Lawless* (Caroline Tyler), *Outcast of Black Mesa* (Ruth Dorn), *Salt Lake Riders* (Helen Thornton), *Frisco Tornado* (Jean Martin).
1951: *Geisha Girl* (Peggy Barnes), *The Kangaroo Kid* (Mary Corbett), *Oriental Evil/The Invisible Mr. Unmei* (Cheryl Banning).
1952: *Wild Stallion* (Caroline Cullen), *Yukon Gold* (Marie).
1953: *Abbott and Costello Go to Mars* (Janie), *So Big* (Paula Hempel).
1954: *Riders to the Stars* (Dr. Jane Flynn), *Lucky Me* (Lorraine Thayer), *The Scarlet Spear* (Christine), *Battle of Rogue River* (Breth McClain), *Sabrina* (Elizabeth Tyson), *Down Three Dark Streets* (Connie Anderson), *Cry Vengeance* (Peggy Harding), *Trouble on the Trail* (kidnapped singer).
1955: *Kiss of Fire* (Felicia), *Francis in the Navy* (Betsy Donevan), *Wyoming Renegades* (Nancy Warren), *Paris Follies of 1956* (Ruth Harmon).
1956: *Red Sundown* (Caroline Murphy), *Showdown at Abilene* (Peggy Bigelow), *Battle Hymn* (Mary Hess).
1957: *Kelly and Me* (Lucy Castle), *Mister Cory* (Abby Vollard), *My Man Godfrey* (Cordelia), *The Delicate Delinquent* (Martha Henshaw).

1958: *Once Upon a Horse* (Miss Amity Babb), *Houseboat* (Carolyn Gibson), *Paris Holiday* (Ann McCall), *Some Came Running* (Gwen French).

1959: *The Big Fisherman* (Herodias), *The Best of Everything* (Barbara Lemont).

1960: *Die Herrin der Welt, Teil 1 und 2/Mistress of the World* (Karin Johansson), *Ice Palace* (Dorothy Kennedy), *Desire in the Dust* (Melinda Marquand).

1961: *The Right Approach* (Anne Perry), *The Last Time I Saw Archie* (Peggy Kramer).

PYRO, 1964 (AIP).

1962: *A Girl Named Tamiko* (Fay Wilson).

1963: *The Man from the Diner's Club* (Lucy), *Wives and Lovers* (Lucinda Ford).

1964: *The Carpetbaggers* (Jennie Denton), *Pyro/Fuego* (Laura Blanco), *Blood on the Arrow* (Nancy Mailer), *First Men in the Moon* (Katherine Callender), *Bikini Beach* (Vivian Clements).

1965: *The Sons of Katie Elder* (Mary Gordon), *Due Marines e un Generale/War Italian Style* (Lt. Inge Schultze).

1966: *The Chase* (Mary Fuller), *The Night of the Grizzly* (Angela Cole), *Cuernavaca en primavera, Picture Mommy Dead* (Francene Shelley).

1967: *The Happening* (Monica), *Some May Live* (Kate Meredith), *Lo Scatenato* (Luisa Chiaramonte), *La Mujer de Otro* (Ana Maria), *House of 1,000 Dolls* (Rebecca).

1969: *Crossplot* (Jo Grinling), *Once You Kiss a Stranger* (Lee).

June Kenney

Pert blonde miss Kenney (sometimes spelled Kenny), was mostly cast in teen-age movies. She was born in Boston around 1935. Before she reached her teens she was active in show business. When she was eleven she moved to California with her family. She became active in school plays and at age fifteen went on tour with a ballet company. June Kenney made her film debut with a small role in Lippert's *Song of Paris* (1952). She did some television shows and had small parts in low-budget movies before she teamed up with director Roger Corman for his *Teenage Doll* (1957) and *Sorority Girl* (1957). In *Attack of the Puppet People* (1958), she is teamed up with John Agar and Laurie Mitchell. They all fall victim to crazy doll seller John Hoyt. He has the power to size them to the format of dolls. The script for this movie was clearly written with Universal's *The Incredible*

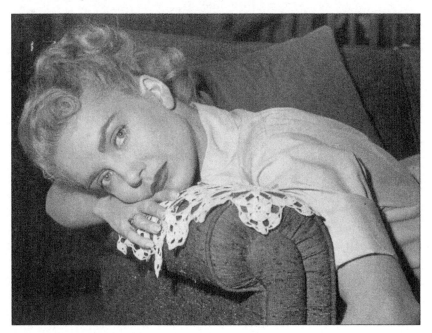

THE SPIDER, 1958 (AIP).

WITH SUSAN CABOT IN *SORORITY GIRL*, 1957 (AIP).

WITH JOHN BRINKLEY IN *TEENAGE DOLL*, 1957 (ALLIED ARTISTS).

Shrinking Man (1957) in mind. Nevertheless, it was entertaining, and, as always, Miss Kenney gave a good performance. Another "copy" movie was the teenage thriller *Earth vs. the Spider* (1958). A small town is menaced by a giant spider that lives in a cave nearby. June and her boyfriend are the brave teenagers who find and fight the spider. The Universal B-movie success of 1955's *Tarantula* clearly influenced the producers of *Earth vs. the Spider*. In the early sixties she returned to television and made her last showbiz appearance in an episode of the Western series, *The Tall Man* in 1962.

WITH JACK HOGAN IN *THE CAT BURGLAR*, 1961 (UNITED ARTISTS).

JUNE KENNEY FILMOGRAPHY

1952: *Song of Paris/Bachelor in Paris* (Jenny Ibbetson), *Has Anybody Seen My Gal?*

1953: *Sweethearts on Parade* (Betty).

1954: *City Story* (teenage girl).

1957: *Teenage Doll* (Barbara Bonney), *Sorority Girl* (Tina), *The Viking Women and the Sea Serpent* (Asmild).

1958: *Attack of the Puppet People* (Sally Reynolds), *Hot Car Girl* (Margaret Dale), *Earth vs. the Spider* (Carolyn Flynn).

1961: *The Ladies Man* (working girl), *The Cat Burglar* (Nan Baker), *Bloodlust!* (Betty Scott).

Barbara Lang

  Maybe MGM starlet Barbara Lang had the shortest movie career of all blondes in this book. As the daughter of silent movie actress/dancer Maureen Knight and Leonidis Bly, she was born Barbara Jean Bly on March 2, 1928, in Pasadena, California. In 1946 she married William McCorkle and had two children. The couple divorced in 1952. Starting out as a nightclub singer and fashion model, she was discovered by a talent scout of MGM studios in 1956 while appearing on television's *Death Valley Days*. In September that year she secretly married *Death Valley Days* co-star Alan Wells in Mexico. Barbara turned down a part in Elvis Presley's *Jailhouse Rock* (1957), because she thought the part wasn't right for her. With Jack Palance she shared some scenes in the prison drama *House of Numbers* (1957). *Picturegoer* magazine wrote about Barbara's performance: "Barbara Lang — who looks as if she's going to behave like an imi-

tator Monroe — attends to her wifely duties with surprising distinction." She was said to be considered by 20th Century-Fox for their production of *The Jean Harlow Story*. Insiders and columnists reasoned that maybe this was a wedge to get Marilyn Monroe to play it. (20th Century-Fox never made this movie. In 1965 Paramount Pictures cast Carroll Baker in the lead of their version of *Harlow*.) After a small part in Cyd Charisse's *Party Girl* (1958), MGM dropped her. Already living separately for over a year, she got her divorce from Alan Wells in November 1958. On January 9, 1959 she was taken to the hospital after taking an overdose of sleeping pills. A few television parts in the late

WITH JACK PALANCE IN *HOUSE OF NUMBERS*, 1957 (MGM).

fifties rounded out her film career. A notable appearance was with Bob Cummings on *The Bob Cummings Show* (1958). Her character in this comedy show was named Doris Monroe. In the sixties she was married for the second time. Her marriage to William J. Otto didn't last either and in 1967 she married for the third time. Barbara appeared regularly on the Broadway stage. She was part of the ensemble and Lee Remick's understudy in *Anyone Can Whistle* (1964),

WITH CYD CHARISSE IN *PARTY GIRL*, 1958 (MGM).

played in the musical *Baker Street* (1965) and had a small part in the musical comedy *The Apple Tree* (1966), with Alan Alda. Barbara was cast with Howard Keel in the non-Broadway play *On a Clear Day You Can See Forever* in 1967. After this play she concentrated on married life, but her third marriage to John George ended in divorce, too, in 1972. She was a regular on the soap *All My Children* (1973). Said to have had an alcohol problem in her later years, Barbara Lang died on July 22, 1982.

BARBARA LANG FILMOGRAPHY

1956: *Hot Summer* Night (girl).
1957: *House of Numbers* (Ruth Judlow).
1958: *Party Girl* (Ginger D'Amour).

Joi Lansing

Born in the sign of Aries, Joy Rae Brown was born on April 6, 1929, in Salt Lake City, Utah. She was the daughter of devout Mormon parents Jack Glenn Brown and Virginia Shupe-Brown. When her parents were divorced, Virginia remarried. Joy adopted the name of her stepfather, Larry Loveland, and at the age of six, the whole family moved to Los Angeles, California. She physically developed early in her teens, so at sixteen she started working as a photographer's model. At seventeen she was briefly married. Soon after the divorce she changed her hair color from brunette to blonde and landed a few bit parts in movies. Her movie debut was in the aptly named Columbia feature *When a Girl's Beautiful* (1947). She was cast under the name of "Joy Loveland." For her role as an art model in *The Counterfeiters* (1948), she called herself "Joyce Lansing." And when MGM producer Arthur Freed spotted her in a high-school play and signed her to a contract, she became "Joy Lansing." With a contract in her hands, Joi really felt things were moving up! But it seemed that the MGM casting directors saw nothing more in her than just a pretty face and figure. After *Neptune's Daughter*, she was dropped by MGM. She went back to modeling for a while. A new acting chance came along in the person of producer/director Hal Roach. He cast her in his short comedy, *Sadie and Sally*, made for television. She played the dumb blonde Sadie. Lois Hall played the wiser Sally. The movie was modeled after the successful short movie series of the thirties that starred blonde Thelma Todd and ZaSu Pitts. When *Life* magazine wrote an article about the upcoming phenomenon of television, they placed Joi on their cover. In the article Roach described Joi as a sort of latter-day combination of Thelma Todd and Jean Harlow. Although the *Life* cover and article were good publicity, it also got her the tag "dumb blonde," a tag she tried to get rid of later in her career. Maybe it was a career move when she married 32 years older Columbia studios' production executive Jerome Safron on March 3, 1950 in Mexico. After four months, Joi filed for a divorce, charging extreme cruelty. Joi was crowned "Miss Hollywood" in 1950 and was considered for a role in MGM's *The Asphalt Jungle*, a part she lost to Marilyn Monroe. In 1951 she married actor Lance Fuller, who remembered his bride as being very ambitious and serious about her career. Maybe they were

WHEN A GIRL'S BEAUTIFUL, 1947 (COLUMBIA).

WITH DOLORES DONLON IN PUBLICITY PHOTO FOR *EASTER PARADE*, 1948 (MGM).

both too involved with their own careers, because the marriage ended unhappily in 1953. Joi herself recalled later: "He was an actor. I paid for his acting lessons, fencing lessons, speech lessons and I don't know what else. But then my money ran out." The early 1950s proved a setback in her movie career. She was only seen in cameo parts in some MGM and RKO musicals (some as a redhead/brunette). From 1954 till 1956 she was a semi-regular in the *Joe McDoakes* short

comedies. These were popular short movies starring comedian George O'Hanlon. They provided Joi with salary beside her modeling and television show appearances. But the part that got her back in the spotlight was that of model Shirley Swanson on TV's *The Bob Cummings Show*. From late 1955 'til September 1959, Joi appeared in 125 of the sitcom's episodes, as the bosomy model that chased after girl-crazy pin-up photographer Bob Cummings. (It was around this time that she changed her name from Joy to Joi.) Casting directors took notice and Joi landed a good role in the Oscar-winning RKO movie *The Brave One*. (The movie wasn't released until late 1956/early 1957.) She also co-starred in two B-movies: *Hot Shots* (1956), a late entry in the once-successful Bowery Boys series, and *Hot Cars* (1956). In the latter, Joi gave a good performance as bad girl Karen Winter. Although this was a B-movie, Joi had the chance to escape her dumb blonde typecasting. The late fifties were a busy time for Joi. She appeared in a couple of movies and was regularly seen in television programs. The highlights from this period were her role in a television movie called *Fountain of Youth* (1958), directed by Orson Welles, and a featured role as Florence Coogle

BUT NOT FOR ME, 1959 (PARAMOUNT).

in Columbia comedy *Who Was That Lady?* (1960), with fellow blonde Barbara Nichols. Around this time it's been said that Joi got romantically involved with Frank Sinatra. (According to author Kitty Kelley, who wrote a notorious Sinatra biography, he paid her medical bills during her final illness.). Nevertheless, Joi married for the third and final time in 1960. Her marriage to producer Stan Todd lasted 'til her death. Todd became her business manager and with no more

PIER 13, 1951 (LIPPERT).

movie offers coming, he arranged some live theatre performances. Also in the early sixties Joi was one of the faces (and voices) for Scopitone. (Scopitone is a kind of jukebox with video clips.) Looking more voluptuous than ever before (it was speculated that Joi got breast implants around this time, which she herself denied), she sang songs like "Web of Love" and "The One I Love Belongs To Somebody Else" in various stages of undress. Joi also recorded an album called *Joi to the World* around this time. In 1966 she was said to be cast in *The Silencers* with Dean Martin. She eventually lost the role to Stella Stevens. In 1967 Joi was cast in the sequel to the Mamie Van Doren/ Jayne Mansfield picture, *Las Vegas Hillbillys*. The movie was called *Hillbillys in a Haunted House* and starred country singer Ferlin Husky. Singers Husky and Lansing are on their way to a Country Music Jamboree, when their car breaks down and they have to stay overnight in an old mansion. The place seems haunted, but is actually the hide-out of some criminals. In the best Scopitone tradition, Joi also sang a couple of songs, like "Gowns, Gowns, Beautiful Gowns." It must be said that Joi had a pleasant, warm

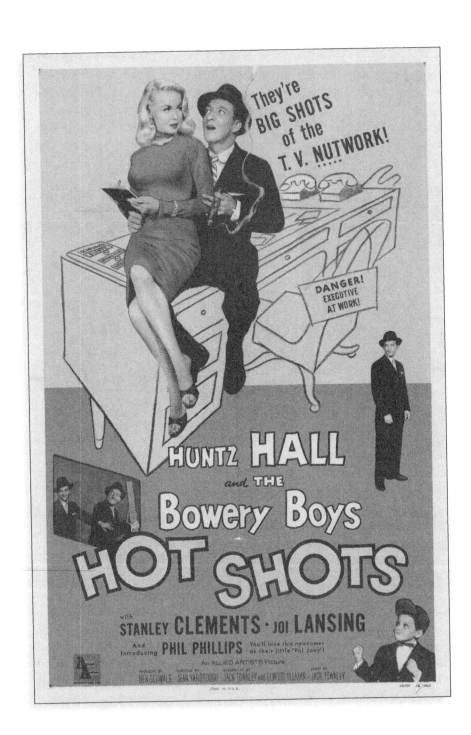

WITH JOHN BROMFIELD IN *HOT CARS*, 1956 (UNITED ARTISTS).

WITH TONY CURTIS, BARBARA NICHOLS AND DEAN MARTIN IN *WHO WAS THAT LADY?*, 1960 (COLUMBIA).

WITH FERLIN HUSKY IN *HILLBILLYS IN A HAUNTED HOUSE*, 1967 (WOOLNER BROTHERS).

WITH MAX BAER JR. IN TV'S *THE BEVERLY HILLBILLIES*, 1967.

and dark voice. The decade was rounded out by occasional appearances on TV's *The Beverly Hillbillies*, as the star-struck Gladys Flatt, and a B-movie called *Bigfoot* (1969). *Bigfoot* was directed by the man who claimed to have been secretly married to Marilyn Monroe, Robert F. Slatzer. In 1968 Joi starred as the gold-digging blonde Lorelei Lee in a 1968 theatre production of *Gentlemen Prefer Blondes*. The show lasted eight weeks. In 1970 she learned that she had a cancerous tumor. She underwent surgery early that summer. On August 7, 1972, Joi Lansing died in a Santa Monica hospital.

JOI LANSING FILMOGRAPHY

1947: *When a Girl's Beautiful* (model), *Linda Be Good* (showgirl).

1948: *Blondie's Secret* (bathing girl in dream), *The Counterfeiters* (art model), *Julia Misbehaves* (mannequin), *Easter Parade* (hat model/showgirl).

1949: *Take Me Out to the Ballgame* (girl on train*)*, *In the Good Old Summertime* (pretty girl), *Neptune's Daughter* (Linda, bathing suit model), *The Girl from Jones Beach* (Randolph girl), *Super Cue Man.*

1950: *Holiday Rhythm* (showgirl).

1951: *F.B.I. Girl* (Susan Matthews), *Pier 23* (cigarette/cocktail girl), *On the Riviera* (Marilyn Turner), *Two Tickets to Broadway* (blonde in boarding house).

1952: *So You Want to Enjoy Life* (secretary), *Singin' in the Rain* (beautiful blonde at party), *Glory Alley* (dance hall girl), *The Merry Widow* (Maxim girl).

1954: *The French Line* (redhead showgirl), *So You Want to Go to a Nightclub* (Homer's girl), *So You're Taking in a Roomer* (Marvin's wife).

1955: *Son of Sinbad* (redhead raider), *So You Want to Be on a Jury*, *So You Want to Be a Vice President*, *So You Want to Be a Policeman* (driver), *The Kentuckian*, *Finger Man* (blonde in bar).

1956: *Terror at Midnight* (Hazel), *So You Think the Grass is Greener* (Geraldine Backspace, beautiful office blonde), *Hot Shots* (Connie Forbes), *Hot Cars* (Karen Winter).

1957: *The Brave One* (Marion Randall).

1958: *Queen of Outer Space* (Larry's girlfriend), *Touch of Evil* (Zita, a stripper).

1959: *A Hole in the Head* (Dorine), *But Not For Me* (beautiful blonde at pool), *It Started with a Kiss* (checkroom girl), *Atomic Submarine* (Julie).

1960: *Who Was That Lady?* (Florence Coogle).

1965: *Marriage on the Rocks* (Lola).

1967: *Hillbillys in a Haunted House* (Boots Malone).

1969: *Bigfoot* (Joi Landis).

Belinda Lee

This beautiful green-eyed British blonde was born in Budleigh Salterton, Devon, England, on June 15, 1935. Her father, Robert Esmond Lee, owned a hotel, and Belinda's mother, Stella Mary Graham, was a florist. She attended the Rookesbury Park Preparatory School in Hampshire and St. Margaret's at Devon. Expressing an interest in acting, she focused on dramatics at the Tudor Arts Academy at Surrey, and then went on to London's Royal Academy of Dramatic Art. Her career as an actress began at he Nottingham Playhouse, where she played in *Daphne Laureola, The Skin Game, The Love of Four Colonels* and *As You Like It*, during 1953 and 1954. She was noticed and signed by the Rank Studio Organization while performing at the Nottingham Playhouse and was groomed in starlet parts. *The Runaway Bus* (1954), with comedian Frankie Howerd and

WITH TOKE TOWNLEY AND MARGARET RUTHERFORD IN *THE RUNAWAY BUS,* 1954 (EROS).

WITH BENNY HILL IN *WHO DONE IT?*, 1956 (RANK).

WITH JACQUES SERNAS IN *LA VENERE DI CHERONEA*, 1958 (FARO FILM).

Margaret Rutherford, was the first. Other movies soon followed. She was one of the students in *The Belles of St. Trinians* (1954) and had a starring role in the low-budget crime movie *Murder by Proxy* (1954) with Dane Clark, which was released in the US as *Blackout*. On June 5, 1954, she married Rank's still photographer, Cornel Lucas. The next year she had a nice role in Norman Wisdoms' *Man of the Moment* (1955). Belinda played a luscious continental film star. In

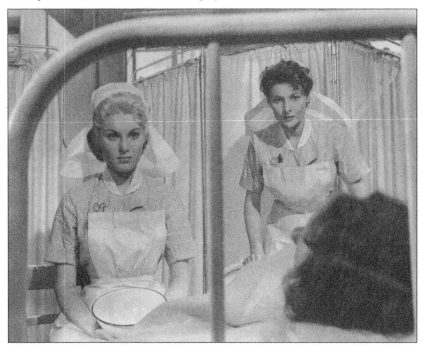

WITH ADRIENNE CORRI IN *THE FEMININE TOUCH*, 1956 (RANK).

1956 she starred with Benny Hill (making his movie debut) in *Who Done It?* and co-starred with Lionel Jeffries in *No Smoking*. *Picturegoer* magazine wrote about Belinda's role in the latter: "Belinda Lee plays a vamp in a wildly extravagant manner." After these comedies Belinda starred in the little thriller *Eyewitness* (1956). *Picturegoer* commented about Belinda's acting, "Belinda Lee doesn't come off so well in uniform, as a conventionally cosy nurse, although it's remarkable how she brings lustre to any old role these days." *The Big Money* (1956) was the next project Belinda was scheduled for. The part of a sexy barmaid in this comedy was originally offered to Diana Dors, who declined. It proved to be the last of Belinda's sexy dumb blonde characters. Being platinum blonde in all of her early films had her being compared to Diana Dors and Sabrina. Because of that her husband advised her to stop bleaching her hair. Belinda turned into a more natural blonde and landed herself some good movie parts in *Miracle in*

Soho and *The Secret Place* (both 1957). British *Photoplay* magazine wrote about the latter: "The attractive Belinda Lee takes another step forward in her bid to gain recognition as a dramatic actress." Belinda then announced shoe would play down the pin-ups and go all out for acting parts: "But by that I don't necessarily mean heavy drama. I simply mean parts, whether serious or gay, with an edge. I want to be much more in films than a kind of animated decoration."

THE SECRET PLACE, 1957 (RANK).

In September 1957 Belinda attended the Venice Film Festival, where she met Prince Filippo Orsini. They were seen all over Venice and Rome together and rumor had it they were having an affair. She soon left England for Italy, where she started a whole new career. In *La Venere di Cheronea* (1958), Belinda played the goddess of love, Aphrodite, and *Le Notti di Lucrezia Borgia* (1959) saw her as the famous medieval seductress. Because his wife was still seeing Orsini and didn't return home, Cornel Lucas filed for a divorce in April 1958. (In June 1959 the divorce became final.) After her last British movie, *Nor the Moon by Night* (1959), Belinda left Rank in December 1958. Together with Orsini, she rented a villa in Munich, Germany. Because he was still married, their relationship was much discussed. (The Pope even intervened; forbidding Orsini to see Belinda.) In January 1960 Belinda ended her relationship with Orsini. She made a couple of movies in Italy, Germany and France. In *Die Wahrheit über Rosemarie* (1959) she played high-class call girl Rosemarie Nitbritt. The film was released in the US as *She Walks By Night*. (A year earlier, German blonde Nadja Tiller played the same character in *Das Mädchen Rosemarie*. This production won the Golden Globe award as "Best Foreign-Language Film.") Belinda looked beautiful in the French-made swashbuckling movie *Marie des Isles* (1960). As the daughter of an innkeeper, she falls in love with a young man (Alain Saury), but has to marry an older colonial official. In Rome she filmed a satirical comedy with Marcello Mastroianni and Sandra Milo, *Fantasmi a Roma* (1961). Belinda played Mastroianni's girlfriend. She went to the United States in 1961 with her new lover, producer/director Gualtiero Jacopetti. Belinda met him while filming *Il Mondo di Notte* (1959), which Jacopetti wrote and narrated. On March 12, they were on their way from Las Vegas to Los Angeles. Because of the high speed, their car got off the road and Belinda was thrown out of the car and killed. Belinda Lee was twenty-six years old. Her premature death robbed the sixties movie world of a talented and beautiful actress.

BELINDA LEE FILMOGRAPHY

1954: *The Runaway Bus* (Janie Grey), *The Case of Canary Jones*, *Meet Mr. Callaghan* (Jenny Appleby), *Life with the Lyons* (Violet Hemingway), *The Belles of St. Trinians* (Amanda), *Murder by Proxy* (Phyllis Brunner).

1955: *Footsteps in the Fog* (Elizabeth Travers), *Man of the Moment* (Sonia), *No Smoking* (Miss Tonkins).

1956: *Eyewitness* (Penny Mander), *Who Done It?* (Frankie Mayne), *The Feminine Touch* (Susan Richards), *The Big Money* (Gloria Lane).

1957: *The Secret Place* (Molly Wilson), *Miracle in Soho* (Julia Gozzi), *Dangerous Exile* (Virginia Traill).

1958: *Nor the Moon by Night* (Alice Lang), *La Venere di Cheronea* (Aphrodite).

1959: *Le Notti di Lucrezia Borgia* (Lucrezia Borgia), *Ce Corps tant désiré* (Lina), *Les Dragueurs* (Ghislaine), *I Magliari* (Paula Mayer), *Die Wahrheit über Rosemarie* (Rosemarie Nitbritt).

1960: *Der Satan lockt mit Liebe* (Evelyn), *Il Sicario*, *Messalina Venere Imperatrice* (Mesallina), *Giuseppe veduto dai Fratelli* (Henet), *Femmine di Lusso* (Adriana Bressan), *Brevi Amori a Palma di Majorca* (Mary Moore), *Marie des Isles* (Marie Bonnard), *La Lunga Notte del '43* (Anna Barilari).

1961: *Fantasmi a Roma* (Eileen).

1962: *Constantino Il Grande* (Fausta).

Carole Lesley

From one of her first appearances before the film cameras blue-eyed Carole Lesley was a star. Literally, she was seen for about three seconds in *The Good Companions* (1956), as a film star arriving at a glittering West End première. She was born Maureen Carole Lesley Rippingdale in Chelmsford, Essex, on May 27 1935. Stimulated by her mother, she landed her first film part in 1947, in adventure movie *The Silver Darlings*. She gained her first stage experience at the age of thirteen when she appeared before an audience of children of her own age, singing and dancing in a Saturday Matinee. Three years later, at the age of sixteen, Carole ran away from home. Determined to enter show business she almost immediately talked her way into a job as a dancer in nightclub cabaret. She also made an uncredited appearance in a small crime movie called *The Embezzler* (1954). Actress Joan Collins saw her at a nightclub, was impressed, and gave Carole her agent's number to ring. Although she said she was scared and not confident about it, she signed with Collins' agent, Bill Watts, anyway. However, she didn't turn up for auditions and interviews arranged by him. "I was scared, but signed with the agent. And then I lost confidence and didn't co-operate. I left the agency and went to Paris where I got a job as a mannequin." Even in Paris, Carole was kicking "Lady Luck" in the face. A top Hollywood agent wanted to interview her, but she didn't turn up. Columbia wanted to give her a test, but she stayed away! When her boyfriend left her for another woman, she felt totally lost and returned to England, settling down in London.

WITH BARBARA MURRAY IN *OPERATION BULLSHINE*, 1959 (ABPC).

WITH JACKIE LANE IN *THESE DANGEROUS YEARS*, 1957 (ABPC).

Gradually she fought against her shyness and lack of confidence: "I wanted people to respect me for myself, so I came home and started to work properly, instead of flitting around the night spot." She changed her name to Leslie Carol and signed on again with Watts. During this period she posed in the nude for photographer Roye. These pictures appeared in a little booklet called *The Art and Beauty Series No. 5* around 1955. (Roye had earlier shot sexy near-nude photos

WITH LESLIE PHILLIPS IN *DOCTOR IN LOVE*, 1960 (RANK).

of Diana Dors for his booklet *Diana Dors in 3-D*.) Carole made some appearances on television's *Yakity-Yak* game show and caught the eye of Robert Lennard, casting director for Associated British Picture Corporation. First she was given a small role in *The Good Companions* (1956) and then ABPC signed her to a seven-year contract. Her next role, *These Dangerous Years* (1957), found her as a teenage near-delinquent, Frankie Vaughan's girlfriend on the tough Liverpool waterfront. *Picturegoer* magazine wrote in its review: "There's Carole Lesley as the little tough-tender backstreets girlfriend. And like (Frankie) Vaughan, she's still raw material, but the star quality is unmistakable." Then in *Woman in a Dressing Gown* (1957) she played the part of a young mother, a neighbor and friend of the main actors, Anthony Quayle and Yvonne Mitchell. Early 1958 she started working on *Ice Cold in Alex*, with John Mills and Anthony Quayle. The role required her to be a brunette. Director J. Lee-Thompson and Carole

WITH JACK WATLING IN *THREE ON A SPREE*, 1961 (UNITED ARTISTS).

herself soon realized this wasn't the role her career needed, and she was replaced by Diane Clare. She was given a small role in Thompson's next project, *No Trees in the Street* (1959) instead. Around this time Carole rivaled Diana Dors in the popularity polls. "The only thing Monroe, Dors and I have in common is that we all like mink. And that's where it ends. I may be classified as the blonde bombshell type, but I'm myself and people will have to get used to Carole Lesley." In the late fifties and early sixties she played in a couple of nice comedies and then all of a sudden disappeared out of the movie business. Occasionally appearing on British television and appearing in pin-up magazines, Carole failed to make a show business return as the movie star she once was. In August 1964 she married Michael Dalling. (In 1966 an actress called Lesley Carole played a small part in a thriller on BBC's *A Game of Murder*. The author doesn't know whether she is actually our Miss Lesley.) Still troubled with lack of confidence and being out of work for a long time, she sadly took her own life on February 28, 1974. Carole Lesley was 38 years old. In September 1956 she said in a *Picturegoer* magazine interview, "I had so little confidence that sometimes I stayed in bed for two or three days just avoiding people. I carried on with the same social crowd — hoping to impress them — hoping that my inferiority complex wouldn't show through the late hours I kept." Carole Lesley was probably the most beautiful of the British blonde stars that graced the silver screen in the fifties.

CAROLE LESLEY FILMOGRAPHY

1947: *The Silver Darlings* (Una as a child).
1949: *Trottie True* (Clare as a child).
1954: *The Embezzler*.
1956: *The Good Companions* (movie star).
1957: *These Dangerous Years* (Dina Brown), *Woman in a Dressing Gown* (Hilda).
1959: *No Trees in the Street* (Lova), *Operation Bullshine* (Pte Marge White).
1960: *Doctor in Love* (Kitten Strudwick).
1961: *What a Whopper!* (Charlie Pinner), *Three on a Spree* (Susan).
1962: *The Pot Carriers* (Wendy).

THE RAINMAKER, 1956 (PARAMOUNT).

Yvonne Lime

Yvonne Lime was born on April 7, 1938, in Glendale, California. She was the daughter of a music teacher who encouraged her to study acting. At age 16 she attended the Pasadena Playhouse and acted in its production of *Ah, Wilderness!* Yvonne Lime attracted the notice of an agent who landed her a recurring part on CBS's television comedy series *Father Knows Best* (1954). She played the part of Dottie Snow from 1954 until 1957. (Also in the cast was fellow teenage actress Sue George.) Making her motion picture debut for Paramount in *The Rainmaker* in 1956, she later played leading roles in B-movies made exclusively for the teenage market. She played the small part of the pregnant teenager Baby, who dies while working in the cotton fields in *Untamed Youth* (1957). The movie that reached cult status was *I Was a Teenage Werewolf* (1957), starring Michael

HIGH SCHOOL HELLCATS, 1958 (AIP).

DRAGSTRIP RIOT, 1958 (AIP).

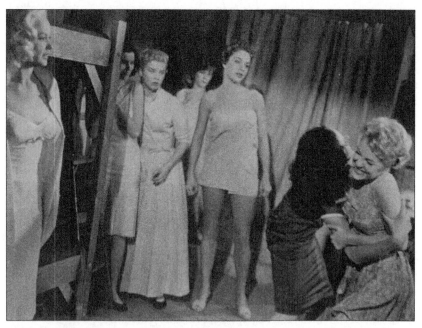

WITH MAMIE VAN DOREN, JEANNE CARMEN AND LORI NELSON IN *UNTAMED YOUTH*, 1957 (WARNER BROS.).

Landon. Opposite Elvis Presley, she was cast in *Loving You* (1957). In *High School Hellcats*, she played Joyce, a new student, who draws the attention of girl gang "The Hellcats." Desperate for acceptance and unhappy with her home life, Joyce goes along with the gang, and is soon drinking, dancing and meeting boys. *Speed Crazy* (1959) was her last movie appearance. She appeared on NBC's comedy *Happy* on television from June 1960 until September 1961, and appeared occasionally on TV until 1968. In March 1969, she married television producer Don Fedderson. They were still married at the time of his death in 1994. She is one of the founders of Childhelp USA, an organization which helps abused and neglected children in the U.S.

I WAS A TEENAGE WEREWOLF, 1957 (AIP).

YVONNE LIME FILMOGRAPHY

1956: *The Rainmaker* (Snookie Maguire).
1957: *Loving You* (Sally), *Untamed Youth* (Baby), *I Was a Teenage Werewolf* (Charlene Logan).
1958: *Dragstrip Riot* (Janet Pearson), *High School Hellcats* (Joyce Martin).
1959: *Speed Crazy* (Peggy Hendrix).

Peggy Maley

Peggy June Maley was born on June 8, 1924, in Pottsville, Pennsylvania. She won the "Miss Atlantic City" competition in 1942, and left for Hollywood the next year. After a couple of uncredited showgirl walk-ons in some musicals, she left Hollywood to play in a Broadway play called *Joy to the World* (1948). The play opened on March 18 at the Plymouth Theatre, and closed 124 performances later, on July 3. In 1949 she dated Al Capone's cousin, Joe Fischetti, and Egyptian King Faruk. Their torrid love affair took her all over Europe. When she returned to Hollywood, she concentrated on modeling and played small roles in movies in the early fifties. During this time she was called a "Lana Turner impersonator." Lana's studio, MGM, used her frequently for their productions. In 1952 she was married to Ricky Rayfield for three months. After her marriage

MAN ON THE PROWL, 1958 (UNITED ARTISTS).

THE GUNS OF FORT PETTICOAT, 1957 (COLUMBIA).

WITH JOAN CAULFIELD AND DAVID NIVEN IN *THE LADY SAYS NO*, 1952 (UNITED ARTISTS).

WITH VAN JOHNSON IN *THE SIEGE AT RED RIVER*, 1954 (20TH CENTURY FOX).

WITH TONY CURTIS IN *THE MIDNIGHT STORY*, 1957 (UNIVERSAL).

WITH CASEY ADAMS IN *THE INDESTRUCTIBLE MAN*, 1956 (ALLIED ARTISTS).

she steadily dated actors like Brad Dexter, Corey Allen and Jason Hall. Being one of Columbia boss Harry Cohn's girlfriends helped her land a contract with that studio. A nice role in Marlon Brando's *The Wild One* (1953) led to nothing substantial and during the mid-fifties she kept on playing featured parts on television and in some B-movies. In *The Indestructible Man* (1956), she and Marian Carr played strippers; in *Escape from San Quentin* (1957) she was Merry Anders sister, and, for her best part in 1957, *The Midnight Story*, she played a gang moll who is manhandled after she gives information to the police. About the importance of getting her name known to the public through pin-up poses, she once commented, "Name value means as much as, or more than, acting ability in Hollywood. If a girl has the luck or equipment to be publicized as glamorous, she'd be a fool to ignore it. I doubt if publicity hurts any career." Peggy Maley's career was rounded out in 1959 with the strange swamp adventure film, *Okefenokee*. The movie was released to the theatres as a double bill with Jeanne Carmen's *Monster of the Piedras Blancas*. Two blondes for the price of one! A lot of television work followed, but in the early sixties she stopped acting and married a man 15 years her junior. (The marriage ended in the mid-seventies.) Nowadays, she lives in California.

PEGGY MALEY FILMOGRAPHY

1943: *A Guy Named Joe* (woman).
1944: *Broadway Rhythm* (autograph seeker), *Meet the People* (showgirl), *Two Girls and a Sailor* (girl), *Since You Went Away*, *Bathing Beauty* (co-ed), *Thirty Seconds over Tokyo* (girl in officers' club).
1945: *Anchors Aweigh* (Lana Turner impersonator).
1946: *The Harvey Girls* (dance hall girl), *The Thrill of Brazil* (showgirl).
1947: *Borrowed Blonde* (pretty blonde neighbor), *Wife Tames Wolf*, *In Room 303* (girl in 303), *Blondes Away* (stenographer), *Down to Earth* (muse).
1951: *I Want You* (Gladys), *The Lady Says No* (Midge).
1953: *Gypsy Colt* (Pat), *The Bigamist* (phone operator), *The Wild One* (Mildred).
1954: *Drive a Crooked Mile* (Marge), *Human Desire* (Jean), *The Siege at Red River* (showgirl Sally).
1955: *Moonfleet* (tavern maid), *I Died a Thousand Times* (Kranmer's girl).
1956: *Meet Me in Las Vegas*, *The Indestructible Man* (stripper Francine).
1957: *The Guns of Fort Petticoat* (Lucy Conover), *Escape from San Quentin*, *The Brothers Rico* (Jean), *The Midnight Story* (Veda Pinelli).
1958: *Tarawa Beachhead* (blonde at bar), *Man on the Prowl* (Alma Doran), *Live Fast, Die Young* (Sue Hawkins), *The Gun Runners* (blonde).
1959: *Okefenokee* (Ricki Hart).

Jayne Mansfield

Ambitious to be a movie star, Vera Jane Palmer came all the way from Dallas to Hollywood, equipped with her natural endowments and the title of "Miss Photoflash of 1952." She arrived as one of hundreds of unknown wannabe actresses in 1954, conquered Broadway and was a well-known Hollywood name two years later! Miss Mansfield was very aware of her physique and the possibilities that it created to establish her name in Hollywood: "If I were flat-chested, people would talk about me. So, if people will talk anyway, I'm glad I've got something big enough for a long conversation." She was born in Bryn Mawr, Pennsylvania, on April 19, 1933. Her father died when she was three years old; her mother married again (to Mr. Peers) and the family moved to Dallas when Jayne was six years old. When she became pregnant at fifteen, she married Paul Mansfield, a fellow high school student. She continued her drama studies and ballet classes, and after graduation she persuaded Paul to go to Hollywood with her. She dyed her brunette hair blonde and knocked at the various studio gates. She got a screen test at Paramount, but they didn't know how to use her. Paul Mansfield didn't like the way his wife transformed and returned home. In January 1955 she went to Florida to help decorate the première of the Jane Russell movie *Underwater*, although she hadn't worked in the film. She got quite some publicity when she "lost" the top of her bathing suit while emerging from the water, and landed a contract at Warner Bros. studios. She was cast in a gangster movie with Edward G. Robinson called *Illegal* (1955). Her performance was compared in many reviews to that of Marilyn Monroe's in *The Asphalt Jungle* (1950). England's *Picturegoer* magazine wrote: "…the blonde they've been buzzing about, Jayne Mansfield, playing the gangster's girlfriend and acting so like Monroe you might almost imagine you were back watching 'The Asphalt Jungle'…" This was the first time that the two blondes were compared (acting wise) to each other. The first time the two blondes met in real life, was on December 2, 1955, at the premiere party for the movie *The Rose Tattoo*. After a couple of other small roles (and a screen test for a part in James Dean's *Rebel Without a Cause*) Jayne was released from her Warner Bros. contract. A starring role in Columbia's *The Burglar* (1956) and the release of her debut film (filmed

WITH CAROL HANEY AND HAL MARCH IN TV'S *THE BACHELOR*, 1956 (NBC).

in 1954 but shelved for two years), *The Female Jungle*, didn't lead to anything new. Her agent suggested that she take a chance in a Broadway play. Although Jayne didn't like the idea, she agreed to star in a play that was a parody on Hollywood. In *Will Success Spoil Rock Hunter?*, she is seen as movie star Rita Marlowe, a caricature of movie star Marilyn Monroe. The play and Jayne in particular became a huge hit. (It ran from October 13, 1955 to November 3, 1956, 444

WITH TOM EWELL IN *THE GIRL CAN'T HELP IT*, 1956 (20TH CENTURY FOX).

performances.) Hollywood showed interest again and she signed a contract with 20th Century-Fox. They rewrote the script of *Rock Hunter* and tested her with the movie-going public in *The Girl Can't Help It* (1956). Jayne was given as co-star Hollywood's finest comic blonde handler, Tom Ewell, who had already supported blondes like Judy Holliday, Marilyn Monroe and Sheree North. She plays a gun moll who is forced to become a star by her lover, Edmond O'Brien. Tom Ewell has to look after her, but gets in trouble when Jayne and he fall in love. *The Girl Can't Help It* is a nice comedy by director Frank Tashlin, with lots of musical numbers by famous (rock 'n roll) artists of that period. The British *Photoplay* magazine reviewed: "As the blonde, Jayne Mansfield is stunning. The film's comedy is centered upon her physical attributes, which gives Tom Ewell plenty of good lines." Jayne's second movie for Fox, *Will Success Spoil Rock Hunter?* (1957), was an excellent movie parody of the advertisement business.

In this movie she repeats her Broadway role and it's probably the most convincing portrayal of her career. She was rushed into *The Wayward Bus* (1957), a drama with Jayne as a girl with a shady past falling in love with fellow bus passenger Dan Dailey. British *Picturegoer* magazine wrote: "A spectacular landslide and a perilous trip across a bridge, straining above a swollen river, are almost as startling as the really expert performances of Joan Collins and Jayne

ILLEGAL, 1955 (WARNER BROS.).

Mansfield." *The Wayward Bus* was followed by the Cary Grant comedy, *Kiss Them for Me* (1957). Jayne looked beautiful in it, but she was mostly cast as decoration. The girl Grant falls for in the movie isn't Jayne, but former model Suzy Parker. Jayne plays a fun-crazy dumb blonde named Alice. While dancing with Grant she whispers in his ear, "Say something sweet to me." Grant replies, "I can say this, you have beautiful hair." "And it's natural; except for the color!" Jayne answers in her typical giggly, squeaky voice. Her last two movies weren't exactly box-office hits and Fox executives didn't show that much interest in her anymore. Jayne was out of work for a while and when she was asked about her prospects for 1958, she answered in her own enthusiastic way, "Sex will be very big next year, I'm glad I am too." Unfortunately, she was big in only one way; which wasn't career wise! 20th Century-Fox no longer thought of Jayne as Hollywood star material. For the duration of her contract (which ended in 1962),

WITH LEIF ERICKSON AND CARY GRANT IN *KISS THEM FOR ME*, 1957 (20TH
CENTURY FOX).

WITH KENNETH MORE IN *THE SHERIFF OF FRACTURED JAW*, 1958 (20TH
CENTURY FOX).

she was loaned out for English (and later Italian) movies. She was granted a divorce from Paul Mansfield on January 8, 1958 and married former Mister Universe Mickey Hargitay five days later. She was send off to Europe to star in *The Sheriff of Fractured Jaw* (1958), which was filmed in Spain, with Kenneth More, and freelanced in a two British movies. *Too Hot to Handle* (1959) had her cast as a nightclub entertainer. Because she wore a transparent sequined

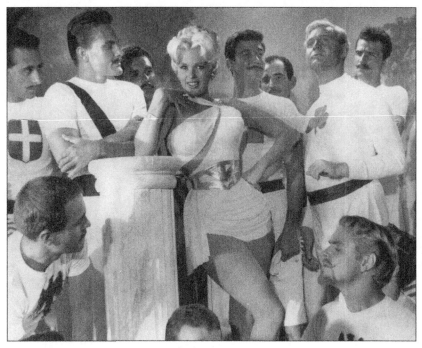

IT HAPPENED IN ATHENS, 1962 (20TH CENTURY FOX).

dress, the movie was refused for American release. (Three years later it was released in the United States under the title *Playgirl After Dark*.) *The Challenge* (1959, U.S. title, *It Takes a Thief*) had her cast as a gang-leader/nightclub singer. Although reliable British actors Carl Mohner and Anthony Quayle starred with Jayne, the movie was again a box office flop. Together with Mickey, she left for Europe's mainland to film *Gli Amori di Ercole* (1960) in Italy. Mickey played Hercules and Jayne had a dual role in this cheap adventure film. Back in the Unites States, 20th Century-Fox loaned her out again for *The George Raft Story* (1961), made by Allied Artists with Ray Danton. Jayne's character of Lisa Lang was modeled after Betty Grable, who had an affair with Raft in her younger days. This was the first time Jayne wore a wig, because her own hair was damaged by the amounts of peroxide it was treated with over the years. Her last film under her Fox contract was *It Happened in Athens* (1962). Most sources say it

BELGIAN POSTER FOR *HEIMWEH NACH ST. PAULI*, 1963.

LOBBY CARD FOR *FEMALE JUNGLE*, 1956 (AMERICAN RELEASING
CORPORATION).

TOO HOT TO HANDLE, 1960 (WARWICK FILMS).

was filmed in 1960, but Fox released it theatrically in June 1962. Jayne plays a glamorous stage actress who promises to marry the winner of the Olympic Games. The movie was partly filmed in Greece, and Jayne never looked lovelier. Her marriage with Hargitay was beginning to fall apart. Although not officially divorced, Jayne was having romances with other men. Between July and December 1962, she was together with the production manager of *Panic Button*, Enrico

SPREE, 1963 (UNITED PRODUCERS RELEASING CORPORATION).

Bomba. And in early 1963 she was seen with Nelson Sardelli, a singer who was in her nightclub acts. On April 30, 1963, Jayne obtained a Mexican divorce from Mickey Hargitay, but by the fall of 1963 Jayne and Mickey were again living together. Their daughter, Mariska Hargitay, was born in January 1964. When Monroe passed away in August 1962, it was assumed that Mansfield would take her throne. Together with Mamie Van Doren and Diana Dors, Jayne was again measured up to Monroe. Jayne commented, "I thought Monroe was a very talented actress. And as far as I know I never took a role Marilyn rejected — such parts weren't even offered to me." The release of her movies from then on varied. She made *Panic Button* in 1962, but it wasn't released in the US until 1964. Her European movies of that period weren't released in the US at all. (*Heimweh nach St. Pauli*, *Dog Eat Dog*, both filmed in 1963 in Germany, and the 1964 Italian-made *Amore Primitivo*.) She still made headlines due to various made-up stunts (e.g., she shipwrecked in the Caribbean), her romances and her totally nude *Playboy* appearance. The *Playboy* layout was shot on location of the low-budget movie *Promises, Promises!* (1963). She was the first well-known American actress to appear nude in a feature film. Tommy Noonan played her husband, and Mickey Hargitay formed a couple with forties blonde, Marie "The Body" McDonald. (Originally, Mamie Van Doren was

LAS VEGAS HILLBILLYS, 1966 (WOOLNER BROTHERS).

asked for the McDonald part. She backed out when she found out that Jayne would receive two-and-a-half percent more of the film's profits.) The flimsy story has all to do with the couples trying to get pregnant and mixing up husbands and wives. It was considered very daring at the time. When there were no further offers, she did some nightclub work, and in the summer of 1964 she and Hargitay did the play *Bus Stop*, directed by Matt Cimber. After the play Jayne left Hargitay and married Cimber on September 24, 1964. The couple made a lot of negative headlines ("Cimber beating Jayne," "Cimber/Hargitay fights") and in 1966 Jayne divorced Matt Cimber. Then MGM cast her for the small part of a travel agency receptionist in *The Loved One* (1965), but her scenes landed on the cutting room floor. Also in 1965, she had a role in country music jamboree, *Las Vegas Hillbillys*. Myth has it that Jayne refused to take part in the scenes with her co-star and blonde rival, Mamie Van Doren; it is said that a double was used in the scenes where they were seen together. Husband Matt Cimber directed Jayne in *Single Room Furnished* (1967). Jayne played three characters in this cheap drama. Filming was completed in the spring of 1966, but it failed to find a distributor, so the movie wasn't released 'til after Jayne's death. December 1966 found her doing a two-minute cameo role in *A Guide For the Married Man* (1967), and in May 1967 *Variety* announced that Jayne had signed to star in *The Ice House* and that filming would start in July of that year. Of course, Jayne never made this movie (British blonde Sabrina was offered the role later), because, on June 29, 1967, she was killed in a car accident near New Orleans on the way to a television engagement. Three of her children were in the back seat of the car and survived the accident miraculously. Jayne's youngest daughter, Mariska Hargitay, became a famous television actress. She's the star of the popular series *Law & Order: Special Victims Unit*. Like Marilyn Monroe, Jayne Mansfield is still very beloved today. Recently a new book about her life and career was written (by Frank Ferruccio) and many websites profiling her career are online today; proving that the public did not lose its interest in this outrageous blonde bombshell!

JAYNE MANSFIELD FILMOGRAPHY

1954: *Female Jungle* (Candy Price).
1955: *Pete Kelly's Blues* (cigarette girl), *Illegal* (Angel O'Hara), *Hell on Frisco Bay* (blonde).
1956: *The Burglar* (Gladden), *The Girl Can't Help It* (Jerri Jordan).
1957: *The Wayward Bus* (Camille), *Will Success Spoil Rock Hunter?* (Rita Marlowe), *Kiss Them for Me* (Alice Krachner).
1958: *The Sheriff of Fractured Jaw* (Kate).
1959: *Too Hot to Handle/Playgirl After Dark* (Midnight Franklin), *The Challenge* (Billy Lacrosse).
1960: *Gli Amori di Ercole/The Loves of Hercules* (Dejaneira/Hipolyte).
1961: *The George Raft Story* (Lisa Lang).
1962: *It Happened in Athens* (Eleni Costa), *Panic Button* (Angela).
1963: *Promises, Promises!* (Sandy Brooks), *Spree* (herself), *Heimweh nach St. Pauli* (Evelyne).
1964: *Dog Eat Dog* (Darlene).
1965: *L'amore Primitivo/Primitive Love* (Jayne), *The Loved One*.
1966: *The Fat Spy* (Junior), *Las Vegas Hillbillys* (Tawni Downs).
1967: *A Guide for the Married Man* (herself), *The Wild, Wild World of Jayne Mansfield* (herself), *Single Room Furnished* (Johnnie, Mae, Eilene).

THE GARMENT JUNGLE, 1957 (COLUMBIA).

Kathy Marlowe

Kathy Marlowe was born, as Kathleen Maslowski, on December 31, 1934, in Minneapolis, Minnesota, of Polish parents. She was a pin-up model who won a job as assistant to photographer Bernard of Hollywood in 1953. "For my part I've never posed in the nude and I always refuse to do semi-nudes. In posing here in Hollywood I've always gone on the old theory that imagination is better than reality. It's certainly been successful for me." Making a name for herself with cheesecake layouts in men magazines and gaining several beauty titles, Kathy signed with Warner Bros. in 1954. After they dropped her in 1955, she freelanced for different studios, playing small movie roles. Besides her movie work Kathy also held a job as a bookkeeper. At Twentieth Century-Fox she was a dance hall hostess and colleague of Jane Russell and Sally Todd in *The Revolt of Mamie Stover* (1956). And in the comedy *The Lieutenant Wore Skirts* (1956), Kathy was seen in a typical Frank Tashlin scene holding two water melons before her breasts. (In Tashlin's *The Girl Can't Help It*, he had Jayne Mansfield holding two milk bottles before her bosom.) In 1958 she received star billing in the independent-made exploitation film *Girl with an Itch*, as sexy tramp Mari Lou Waverly. When hitchhiker Mari Lou gets a ride from farm owner Robert Armstrong, she romances him to secure her future. But because of her flirting with his son (Robert Clarke) and their farmhand (Scott Douglas), she spoils this plan and ends up with nothing. A reviewer for *The Motion Picture Exhibitor* wrote: "Miss Marlowe is a voluptuous blonde, bursting at the seams in the one dress that displays most of her charms throughout the picture." She also appeared on television in *Love That Bob*, appearing as one of Robert Cummings' models, in the season 1957-1959. On June 21, 1959 she married actor Harry Jackson. In 1961 the couple separated and their divorce became final on March 14, 1962. Her last movie role was in the all-female Western, *Five Bold Women* (1960), with fellow blondes Merry Anders and Irish McCalla. After a couple of television appearances, she quit show business in 1961. She eventually set up "The Kathy Marlowe Charm School."

THE GIRL WITH AN ITCH, 1958 (DONTRU PRODUCTIONS).

KATHY MARLOWE FILMOGRAPHY

1952: *The Big Trees* (Daisy's girl), *The Winning Team* (box office dame).

1954: *The Bounty Hunter* (Mrs. Ed), *The Human Jungle* (Vody).

1955: *Women's Prison* (inmate), *Illegal* (Gloria Benson), *Sudden Danger* (model), *The Phenix City Story* (Mamie).

1956: *The First Traveling Saleslady* (model), *The Lieutenant Wore Skirts* (Gloria), *The Revolt of Mamie Stover* (Zelda), *Carousel* (extra), *Back from Eternity* (extra).

1957: *Bombers B-52* (blonde at bar), *The Helen Morgan Story* (girl at bar), *The Sad Sack*, *The Garment Jungle* (fitting model), *The Pajama Game* (Holly), *Death in Small Doses.*

1958: *Rock-a-Bye Baby* (secretary), *Queen of Outer Space* (Venus girl), *Girl with an Itch* (Mari Lou Waverly).

1959: *Career* (blonde).

1960: *Five Bold Women* (Faro Kitty).

Irish McCalla

Former Varga girl Irish McCalla reached her peak of fame when she starred on television as *Sheena, Queen of the Jungle*, in 1955. She was born Irish Elizabeth McCalla, on Christmas Day, 1928, in Pawnee City, Nebraska. Her Irish/French parents had seven other children. At the age of eighteen she visited Los Angeles with her brother. She decided to stay and landed herself a job as a waitress. In 1951 she married insurance man Patrick McIntyre. Together, they had two children. Her showbiz break came when she was spotted at Santa Monica beach by a group of officers who were screening contestants for the title of "Miss Navy Day." She won the title and decided to try modeling as a career. Irish became a famous pin-up model before she did any TV or film work; appearing in dozens of magazine layouts. About her sex appeal, Irish once told the press: "One thing men like about me is that I´m sexy looking and yet look like I could live next door." In 1955

WITH TOD GRIFFIN AND VICTOR SEN YUNG IN *SHE DEMONS*, 1958 (ASTOR PICTURES).

she did a screen test (together with buxom blonde Anita Ekberg) for a new TV series called *Sheena, Queen of the Jungle*. She turned blonde for her part of Sheena and kept it that way in her other films. In 1957 she divorced Patrick McIntyre. During the fifties she made a handful of cheap B-movies. A cult favorite these days is the cheaply-made *She Demons* (1958), from director Richard E. Cunha. He also gave us the terrible *Frankenstein's Daughter* (1958, with Sally Todd) and

WITH KATHY MARLOWE IN *FIVE BOLD WOMEN*, 1960 (CITATION FILMS).

Missile to the Moon (1959, with Tania Velia, Sandra Wirth and Marjorie Hellen) and directed Jayne Mansfield in *Dog Eat Dog* (1963). After a small part as a brunette in *The Beat Generation* (1959), Irish appeared as a nun in *Five Gates to Hell* (1959). Her last motion picture was *Hands of a Stranger* (1962). It was filmed in 1960, but shelved for two years. In 1963 she quit acting after her divorce from second husband, actor Patrick Horgan, whom she married in 1958. In 1969 and 1981 she overcame a brain tumor. Irish McCalla eventually did die from a brain tumour and stroke complications on February 1, 2002, in Tucson, Arizona.

IRISH McCALLA FILMOGRAPHY

1952: *River Goddesses*.
1958: *She Demons* (Jerrie Turner).
1959: *The Beat Generation* (Marie Baron), *Five Gates to Hell* (Sister Magdalena).
1960: *Five Bold Women* ("Big" Pearl Jackson).
1962: *Hands of a Stranger* (Holly).

SUNDAY ⬛ NEWS
NEW YORK'S PICTURE NEWSPAPER
COLOROTO MAGAZINE   April 25, 1954
10¢

Beverly
Michaels

Beverly Michaels

B-movie actress Beverly Michaels was born in New York City, on December 29, 1928, as one of the six children of Denzil and Catherine Michaels. Being very tall for her age, the young girl started fashion modeling at the age of nine and won a newspaper beauty contest at eleven. At sixteen she started out as a showgirl, working at the Billy Rose's Diamond Horseshoe and other nightclubs. Beverly made her stage debut in *Glad to See You*, a play with Jane Withers. It opened November 13, 1944, in Philadelphia, and closed on January 6, 1945, at the Boston Opera House, cancelling the scheduled Broadway opening. The money she earned as a showgirl and Conover model was spent on drama study in 1945. Now caught by the acting virus, she left for Hollywood in

WITH VAN HEFLIN IN *EAST SIDE, WETS SIDE*, 1949 (MGM).

WITH HOWLAND CHAMBERLIN IN *PICKUP*, 1951 (COLUMBIA).

WITH EVELYN SCOTT IN *WICKED WOMAN*, 1953 (UNITED ARTISTS).

1948. Her height (5'9") got her cast in MGM's *East Side, West Side* (1949) as "the tall girl," bad blonde Felice Backett. Her part was a key role in the movie, because it was she who had murdered Ava Gardner. In September 1949, Beverly married the movie's producer, Voldemar Vetluguin, who was about 30 years her senior. The next year the couple had already separated. After a small part at MGM she found herself out of work for a while. But when actor/director/

WITH PAUL SAVAGE IN *BETRAYED WOMEN*, 1955 (ALLIED ARTISTS).

producer Hugo Haas needed a scheming blonde for his self-written drama, *Pickup* (1951), he cast Beverly. She played wicked showgirl Betty Horak, and the movie was advertised with taglines like: "The low-down on a come-on girl." Elderly widower Haas marries unscrupulous blonde Michaels who quickly get tires of life at the lonely railway stop where he works. She tries to lure her lover (Allan Nixon) into murdering Haas. Because *Pickup* was a commercial success, Haas rushed her into a second drama, *Girl on the Bridge*, that same year. The next year Haas replaced her with Cleo Moore in his movies. Beverly had a small role in a Bowery Boys comedy that year, and again found herself out of movie work. In late 1952 she met and romanced director/producer Russell Rouse, sang Christmas carols at a USO tour in Alaska and announced her intention of marrying Rouse after the USO tour. They were not to be married for the next few years, but Rouse did write the screenplay for her next movie, *Wicked Woman* (1953), which was distributed by United Artists. As Billie Nash, a scheming bad blonde, she attempts to steal bar owner Richard Egan from his alcoholic wife. Her attempt nearly succeeds. A couple of prison movies followed. *Crashout* (1955) meant a nice role for Beverly, as the woman who

BLONDE BAIT, 1956 (ASSOCIATED FILM RELEASING CORPORATION).

unwillingly hides some escaped inmates on her farm and falls in love with one of them (Arthur Kennedy). *Betrayed Women* (1955) had her imprisoned herself. Together with tough cookie Carole Mathews, she plans to escape, taking Peggy Knudsen and Tom Drake with them as hostages. Beverly then went to Britain to star in a low-budget prison movie again. *Women Without Men* (1956) had her cast as showgirl Angie Booth, who is wrongly accused of murder and is set free from prison to be used as bait to capture the real murderer. *Women Without Men* was released in the US as *Blonde Bait*. For the US version, they re-shot some scenes with American actors (Jim Davis took the male lead) and changed the storyline somewhat. After a television appearance in Hitchcock's "The Big Switch" and two *Cheyenne* episodes called "The Storm Riders" (which was released in Europe as a feature film in 1956), Beverly disappeared from the movie scene when she married her long-time fiancé Russell Rouse around 1957. She gave birth to two sons in 1958 and 1961 respectively. In 1987 she became Rouse's widow when he passed away at the age of 73. Living a secluded life for over 50 years, Beverly Michaels died on June 2007, in Phoenix, Arizona, after a stroke.

BEVERLY MICHAELS FILMOGRAPHY

1949: *East Side, West Side* (Felice Backett).

1950: *Three Little Words* (shipboard woman).

1951: *Pickup* (Betty Horak), *The Girl on the Bridge* (Clara).

1952: *No Holds Barred* (blonde at party), *The Marrying Kind* (blonde on *Life* magazine cover).

1953: *Wicked Woman* (Billie Nash).

1955: *Betrayed Women* (Honey Blake), *Crashout* (Alice Mosher).

1956: *Women Without Men/Blonde Bait* (Angela Booth), *The Storm Riders* (Sheila Dembro).

Marjie Millar

Marjie Millar was born Marjorie Joy Miller on August 10, 1930, in Tacoma, Washington. At the age of five she won a Shirley Temple look-alike contest in her hometown and was chosen as the first drum majorette for the Afifi Temple band. At eleven she entertained the soldiers at Fort Lewis with a song-and-dance routine and while in high school she starred in the theatre play *Janie* (1948). In 1952 she left Tacoma for Los Angeles and soon afterwards was crowned "Miss Hollywood Star of 1952." She had a promising start to her career when she signed a contract at Paramount studios in 1953 and starred in *Money from Home*, starring Dean Martin and Jerry Lewis, and *About Mrs. Leslie* (1954). At the 1954 presentation of the Academy Awards, she and starlet Sara Shane modeled the costumes that were nominated for the Oscar.

WITH RAYMOND GREENLEAF IN *WHEN GANGLAND STRIKES*, 1956 (REPUBLIC).

Fondly —
Marjie Millar

She was titled "a promising newcomer" and did some television (most notably playing the character of Susan in 28 episodes of the Ray Bolger show, *Where's Raymond?*, which aired in 1954) and played a starring role in Republic's *When Gangland Strikes* (1956). On April 23, 1955, she had married television producer John Florea. A car accident in 1957 left her partly crippled. Marjie was forced to give up her acting career and returned to her hometown after her divorce from Florea in 1958. On April 16, 1966, she died from complications of sixteen separate leg operations.

WITH ALEX NICOL IN *ABOUT MRS. LESLIE*, 1954 (PARAMOUNT).

MARJIE MILLAR FILMOGRAPHY

1953: *Money from Home* (Phylis Leigh).
1954: *About Mrs. Leslie* (Nadine Roland).
1956: *When Gangland Strikes* (June Ellis).

Magda Miller

Magdalena Ekaterina Antonina Vishinski Klastaites was born in Strathblane, Scotland, in 1934. She's of Scottish, Russian and Lithuanian descent. She was ten when she was run over by a truck. She spent the next year in the hospital, recovering from internal injuries. At sixteen she started to enter beauty contests and at the age of eighteen she had already won thirty-six beauty titles, including "Miss Scotland." She was offered contracts to appear in a Follies Bergere show at the Paris Lido by French talent scouts, but Magda used the prize money to study at the Academy of Dramatic Arts in Edinburgh. "I did it all for money. I even turned down beauty titles if there was no money offered for the prize. It wasn't the publicity I was after. I needed the cash to pay for my dramatic

WITH MARSHALL THOMPSON IN *THE SECRET MAN*, 1958 (BUTCHER'S FILM DISTRIBUTORS).

WITH RHODES REASON IN *MAN-EATER*, 1957 (BEACONSFIELD PRODUCTIONS).

lessons." One thing led to another and from repertory (a small part in the West End play *Ring Out the Bells*, 1953), Magda finally stepped into small television roles. Then Magda's luck took a nasty dive. She was ill for two years; she hadn't completely recovered from the truck accident. Her first film, after she got out of the hospital, was the comedy *It's Never Too Late* (1955). More sexy blonde parts followed, but Magda confessed she wanted more out of her acting career: "Theatre producers seem scared of blondes. They think they are not serious enough for Shakespeare. But I'll show them!" As a blackmailing blonde, she was murdered in *Behind the Headlines* (1956). Her next movie character was about to meet the same fatal ending. She got quite some attention with her role in *Town on Trial* (1957), in which she plays the fast-paced, fun-loving good-time girl, Molly Stevens, who meets trouble halfway and ends up dead! It was her image that dominated all posters and publicity material. After another featured part in *Let's Be Happy* (1957), she received the female lead in the adventure movie *Man-Eater* (1957). The movie was made from a couple of episodes of a television series called *White Hunter*. Magda played a spoiled millionaire's daughter, on safari with her alcoholic husband (Lee Patterson), who starts flirting with the game hunter (Rhodes Reason) who leads them around the jungle. With no more movie parts offered to her, she switched to the small screen. On British television she was kept quite busy during the sixties and seventies. Magda is well remembered for her recurring role as Mimi in the comedy/children's series *Tottering Towers*, which ran for 13 episodes in the 1971-1972 season. I wonder where Miss Miller is now...

MAGDA MILLER FILMOGRAPHY

1955: *It's Never Too Late, Dollars for Sale* (girl).
1956: *The Silken Affair* (secretary), *Behind the Headlines* (Nina Duke).
1957: *Town on Trial* (Molly Stevens), *Let's Be Happy* (Mrs. MacTavish),
     Man-Eater (Betty Carver Latham).
1958: *The Truth about Women, The Secret Man* (Ruth).
1960: *The Two Faces of Dr. Jekyll* (US: *House of Fright*) (Sphinx girl).

Laurie Mitchell

Although many think blonde Zsa Zsa Gabor was *Queen of Outer Space* (1958), it was Laurie Mitchell who played the title role of disfigured queen Yllana. Before she starred in this science-fiction cult stinker, she played minor parts in B-movies. She was born Mickey Koren, in Brooklyn, New York, around 1929. In her early teens she modeled fashion and won several beauty titles. When Laurie and her family moved to Los Angeles she met and married trumpeter Larry White at age 21. As Barbara White she did some plays on stage and had a small movie part in *All About Eve* (1950) with a young Marilyn Monroe. She switched to the professional name Laurie Mitchell around 1954. After some cameo parts, Laurie got the part of mean prison inmate Phyllis in *Girls in Prison* (1956). She

WITH HELEN GILBERT, ADELE JERGENS AND MAE MARSH IN *GIRLS IN PRISON*, 1956 (AIP).

WITH ANGIE DICKINSON IN *CALYPSO JOE*, 1957 (ALLIED ARTISTS).

WITH SCOTT PETERS, SUSAN GORDON, KEN MILLER, JUNE KENNEY AND JOHN AGAR IN *ATTACK OF THE PUPPET PEOPLE*, 1958 (AIP).

shares some scenes with forties blonde Adele Jergens. An entry in the *Bowery Boys'* series, *Fighting Trouble* (again with Jergens), followed that same year. In 1957 she gave birth to a daughter and had a busy year working for television and appearing in four movies. Switching between bit parts and featured roles, Laurie ended the fifties with a small role in another Marilyn Monroe movie, *Some Like it Hot.* She was seen as Mary Lou, the trumpet player in Sweet Sue's all-girl band. In the sixties she turned brunette and was seen mostly in television films. She ended her career in 1968. Remarried, Laurie Mitchell resides in the Los Angeles area.

LAURIE MITCHELL FILMOGRAPHY

1950: *All About Eve.*
1954: *20,000 Leagues Under the Sea* (girlfriend).
1955: *Women's Prison* (inmate), *The Rawhide Years.*
1956: *Girls in Prison* (Phyllis), *Fighting Trouble* (Dolly Tate).
1957: *The Garment Jungle* (fitting model), *The Oklahoman* (girl), *Calypso Joe* (Leah, a stewardess), *The Helen Morgan Story* (showgirl).
1958: *The Female Animal* (manicurist), *Attack of the Puppet People* (Georgia Lane), *Queen of Outer Space* (Queen Yllana), *Missile to the Moon* (Lambda).
1959: *Some Like it Hot* (Mary Lou, trumpet player).
1960: *Hell Bent for Leather.*
1962: *That Touch of Mink* (showgirl).
1963: *A New Kind of Love* (Parisienne poule), *Gunfight at Comanche Creek* (Tina Neville).
1965: *Runaway Girl* (Winnie Bernay).
1966: *Lord Love a Duck* (Jack's wife).

Marilyn Monroe

What more can be told about Marilyn Monroe? Over the 40 years since she passed away there have been numerous articles, books, documentaries about her. She must be the most written about movie star in all of film history. She is the inspiration of this book and was the inspiration of many of the ladies included in these chapters. Norma Jean Baker was born on June 1, 1926, in Los Angeles. Her father left when she was a baby, leaving her mother Gladys to take care of her. "Success came to me in a rush. It surprised my employers much more than it did me. Even when I had played only bit parts in a few films, all the movie magazines and newspapers started printing my picture and giving me write-ups. I used to tell lies in my interviews — chiefly about my father and mother. I'd say she was dead and he was somewhere in Europe. I lied because I was ashamed to have the world to know my mother was in a mental institution — and that I had

WITH ADELE JERGENS IN *LADIES OF THE CHORUS*, 1948 (COLUMBIA).

been born 'out of wedlock' and never heard my illegal father's voice." With her mother in a mental institution, young Norma Jean was raised in several orphanages and by different foster parents. The young girl dreamt of becoming a movie star and at age seventeen she started out as a model. She was very much in demand during the forties. Married at sixteen (to James Dougherty) and divorced in 1946, she was signed by 20th Century-Fox in 1947, making two films for them.

WITH GROUCHO MARX IN *LOVE HAPPY*, 1949 (UNITED ARTISTS).

The first one to reach the theatres was a little crime drama called *Dangerous Years* (1947). But her original debut was in *Scudda Hoo! Scudda Hay!* (1948). The few lines she spoke in this movie ended up on the cutting room floor. There has been speculation that Marilyn had cameo parts in other Fox movies of that period. It was said she was seen as a telephone operator in *The Shocking Miss Pilgrim* (1947) and that she played a dancer in *You Were Meant for Me* (1948). (Other possible movies mentioned are *Mother Wore Tights* [1947], *The Challenge* and *Green Grass of Wyoming*, both 1948.) When she was dropped by Fox, her agent Johnny Hyde landed her a starring role in the B-musical *Ladies of the Chorus* (1948) at Columbia with Adele Jergens. Marilyn played Miss Jergens' daughter in this story of back-stage romance, which was made in eleven days. The role didn't go unnoticed by the press, but nevertheless it was back to cameo parts in small films. She also turned to modeling again, working for photographers André de Dienes and Tom Kelley. It was the latter who persuaded Marilyn to pose in the nude. She

AS YOUNG AS YOU FEEL, 1951 (20TH CENTURY FOX).

WE'RE NOT MARRIED, 1952 (20TH CENTURY FOX).

only agreed because she needed the money to pay the rent. A walk-on part in United Artists' *Love Happy* (1949) saw her as a client at Groucho Marx's detective bureau. Her one and now famous line in that movie was: "Some men are following me, and I don't know why..." Together with three other fellow starlets she sang "Oh, What a Forward Young Man You Are'" to Dan Dailey in *A Ticket to Tomahawk* (1950). Then Fox picked her up again. Agent and lover Johnny

WITH ZACHARY SCOTT IN *LET'S MAKE IT LEGAL*, 1951 (20TH CENTURY FOX).

Hyde had arranged two good parts in *The Asphalt Jungle* and *All About Eve* (both 1950), and Fox executives saw star potential in the sexy blonde. Her new contract gave her the opportunity to vary her dumb blonde roles in a couple of pleasant comedies. Sometimes she was a secretary, a seductress or beauty contest winner. RKO borrowed her to play the juvenile lead in *Clash by Night* (1952). Because of the role and the enthusiasm of the critics, her status improved phenomenally. 20th Century-Fox gave her a strong role in their suspense thriller, *Niagara* (1953). As the scheming wife of Joseph Cotten, Marilyn meets a gruesome end by his hands. *Time* magazine commented about Marilyn's performance: "What lifts the film above the commonplace is its star, Marilyn Monroe." While filming *Niagara*,

WITH JANE RUSSELL IN PUBLICITY PHOTO FOR *GENTLEMEN PREFER BLONDES*, 1953 (20TH CENTURY FOX).

it was discovered that she had posed for a nude calendar some three years earlier. This made headlines; and the world laughed at her answer when asked whether she had anything on at all: "Yes, the radio." Her comments to the press, her public appearances and the photographs had sold her to the public in a bigger way than any publicity machine could have devised. Maybe all this was just a built-up to the role of ultimate dumb blonde Lorelei Lee, in *Gentlemen Prefer Blondes* (1953).

WITH TOM EWELL IN *THE SEVEN YEAR ITCH*, 1955 (20TH CENTURY FOX).

The role was intended for Fox queen Betty Grable, but her fee was more then ten times Marilyn's. So Marilyn got her chance and took it! The movie and Marilyn became a huge hit. Fox rushed her into another dumb blonde role in *How to Marry a Millionaire* (1953). In it she plays a model who shares an apartment with model friends Lauren Bacall and Betty Grable, who are all trying to catch a millionaire, but end up with true romance at the end of the film. The expected rivalry between Miss Grable and Marilyn wasn't shown during filming. In later accounts Marilyn told the press that Miss Grable was very nice to her. Her next movie, *River of No Return* (1954), and the ones she was planned for were not to Monroe's liking; she started to revolt against the parts offered her. In January 1954 she had married baseball player Joe DiMaggio and while on honeymoon, Fox contracted Sheree North to threaten Monroe. They told her that Sheree would fill in the roles Monroe declined. Marilyn only accepted *There's No Business Like Show Business* (1954), though she disliked the script and her part, because she

WITH TONY CURTIS IN *SOME LIKE IT HOT*, 1959 (UNITED ARTISTS).

WITH LAURENCE OLIVIER IN *THE PRINCE AND THE SHOWGIRL*, 1957 (WARNER BROS.)

was allowed to play in *The Seven Year Itch* afterwards. Marilyn gave a fine performance as the girl from upstairs. She befriends her neighbor Tom Ewell while his wife is out of town. He dreams of a romance with her, while she's just enjoying his company and friendship. It was the ultimate dumb blonde part. Marilyn's blowing skirt scene was the highlight of the movie, creating much publicity even before the movie was released to the public. After the completion of *The Seven*

LET'S MAKE LOVE, 1960 (20TH CENTURY FOX).

Year Itch (1955), Marilyn formed her own production company with photographer Milton Greene. She told the press: "I don't want to play sex roles anymore. I'm tired of being known as the girl with the shape." Fox had to give in to her and cast her in *Bus Stop* (1956). The movie tells the tale of an untalented second-rate singer, Cherie, who falls in love with an innocent cowboy (Don Murray). The press raved about Marilyn's acting and wrote that she finally proved herself an actress. *The Los Angeles Examiner* wrote: "This is Marilyn's show, and, my friend, she shows plenty in figure, beauty and talent. The girl is a terrific comedienne as the bewildered little 'chantoose' of the honky-tonk circuit." She married intellectual writer Arthur Miller on June 29, 1956. (Her marriage to DiMaggio ended after nine months, because he couldn't accept the sexy roles his wife was playing. The blowing skirt scene from *The Seven Year Itch* especially upset him.) When Marilyn left for England to film *The Prince and the Showgirl*, for Warner Bros.

THERE'S NO BUSINESS LIKE SHOW BUSINESS, 1954 (20TH CENTURY FOX).

with Laurence Olivier, Fox tried to put British Diana Dors under contract. When she declined they settled for the new blonde sensation Jayne Mansfield. They gave her a seven-year contract. But the public stood by Marilyn and Fox had to realize there was no replacement for the irreplaceable. About her blonde contemporaries Marilyn once said, "Sometimes I kid the fans. They say, 'Oh you're Marilyn Monroe!' I say, 'Oh no, I'm Mamie Van Doren' or 'Sheree North,' if I'm

WITH THELMA RITTER IN *THE MISFITS*, 1961 (UNITED ARTISTS).

in a real hurry!" Marilyn didn't make a movie throughout 1958. She wanted the part Maria Schell played in *The Brothers Karamazov* (1958) and lost the part in Paddy Chayefsky's *Middle of the Night* (1959) to Kim Novak. 1959 didn't have her back at Fox either (they wanted her to star in *The Blue Angel*, but when she refused, Swedish newcomer May Britt played the part); instead, she signed for a picture with United Artists. *Some Like It Hot* (1959) is, of course, the ultimate Monroe movie. Filmed in black and white and set in the Roaring Twenties, Marilyn was cast as ukulele player Sugar Kane. On tour with an all-girl band, she befriends Tony Curtis and Jack Lemmon who are on the run from gangsters. They pretend to be girl musicians, which leads to hilarious moments in this comedy classic. Director Billy Wilder got the best out of her, although he had a very hard time doing so. Marilyn was often late on the set and forgot her lines; so many scenes had to be done over and over. Nevertheless, *Some Like It Hot* is the top moneymaking and most successful film of Marilyn's career. At Fox, *Let's*

BELGIAN POSTER FOR *DON'T BOTHER TO KNOCK*, 1952 (20TH CENTURY FOX).

Make Love (1960) was of another order. It's a poor showbiz tale of love between an actress and a millionaire (Yves Montand). Director George Cukor commented later that Marilyn had difficulty concentrating. Her reliance on sleeping pills and stimulants was by now well known. While her marriage with Miller was falling apart, she starred in a movie especially written for her by her husband. The film was *The Misfits* (1961), with Clark Gable and Montgomery Clift. The movie was not a financial success. Before the release of *The Misfits*, Marilyn divorced Arthur Miller on November 11, 1960. Marilyn was frequently hospitalized in psychiatric clinics. Former husband Joe DiMaggio gave her much support during this period. Her last assignment was at Fox again. *Something's Got to Give* (1962) was the prophetic title of the movie that proved to be Marilyn's last. Although it was never finished, the scenes that were shot show a lovely, vulnerable Marilyn. Co-star Dean Martin later said she made a sprightly impression. Maybe this is one of the reasons that her suicide on August 5, 1962 is doubted by many. A week before her death she had told *Life* magazine: "I never understood it — this sex symbol — I always thought symbols were things you clash together. That's the trouble, a sex symbol becomes a thing — I just hate being a thing."

MARILYN MONROE FILMOGRAPHY

1947: *Dangerous Years* (Eve).
1948: *Scudda Hoo! Scudda Hay!* (girlfriend), *Ladies of the Chorus* (Peggy Martin).
1949: *Love Happy* (Groucho Marx' client).
1950: *A Ticket to Tomahawk* (Clara), *The Asphalt Jungle* (Angela Phinlay), *The Fireball* (Polly), *All About Eve* (Miss Casswell), *Right Cross* (girl in club).
1951: *Home Town Story* (Iris Martin), *As Young as You Feel* (Harriet), *Love Nest* (Roberta Stevens), *Let's Make it Legal* (Joyce Mannering).
1952: *Clash by Night* (Peggy), *We're Not Married* (Annabel Norris), *Don't Bother to Knock* (Nell Forbes), *Monkey Business* (Lois Laurel), *O. Henry's Full House* (streetwalker).
1953: *Niagara* (Rose Loomis), *Gentlemen Prefer Blondes* (Lorelei Lee), *How to Marry a Millionaire* (Pola Debevoise).
1954: *River of No Return* (Kay Weston), *There's No Business Like Show Business* (Vicky).
1955: *The Seven Year Itch* (the girl).
1956: *Bus Stop* (Cherie).
1957: *The Prince and the Showgirl* (Elsie Marina).
1959: *Some Like it Hot* (Sugar Kane).
1960: *Let's Make Love* (Amanda Dell).
1961: *The Misfits* (Roslyn Tabor).

HOLD BACK TOMORROW, 1955 (UNIVERSAL).

Cleo Moore

Cleo Una Moore was born on Halloween in Baton Rouge, capitol of Louisiana, on October 31, 1928. In 1945, within a few years of graduation, Cleo married Palmer Long (the youngest son of then-Louisiana governor Huey Long). Their marriage only lasted six weeks. In 1946 Cleo and her family headed for Southern California. Cleo soon settled in Hollywood, determined to become a movie star. After a small part in Warners' *Embraceable You* (1948), she landed herself the leading lady part in a Columbia serial, *Congo Bill* (1948). She played Ruth Culver, the heiress of a fortune who is sought after by Congo Bill (Don McGuire). He eventually finds her in the jungle, where she is known as Queen Lureen to the natives. In late 1949 she was under contract at Warner Bros. Studios. While attending a boxing match at the Hollywood Legion Stadium, she was seen by a talent scout from RKO, with the result that she launched herself a contract with that studio. They gave her a bigger build-up then Warners did. To get rid of her Southern accent, Cleo studied voice with vocal coach Josephine Dillon, who was Clark Gable's first wife. Cleo won a lot of beauty titles and appeared in many magazines and newspapers from that time. Her best performance from that period came with Nicholas Ray's *On Dangerous Ground* (1952), a *film noir* classic. Cleo shared a sexy scene with Robert Ryan and received some good reviews from the press. B-movie actor/director/producer and screenwriter Hugo Haas was also impressed by her performance. He signed her to star in his melodramatic *Strange Fascination* (1952), a Columbia Pictures release, casting her as a sexy blonde model/dancer who becomes the obsession of a famous pianist (Haas). Their romance eventually destroys his career. Due to the success of the movie, Cleo replaced Haas' former star actress, Beverly Michaels, as the leading lady in his movies. In their next production, *One Girl's Confession* (1953) for Columbia, Cleo is a waitress who steals the money back that her boss had stolen from her father. She confesses to her crime, serves time in prison and comes out a reformed girl! Marilyn Monroe's studio, 20th Century-Fox, took her in for a two-picture deal. *Thy Neighbor's Wife* (1953) was a period piece with Cleo as an adulteress who is sentenced to death by her husband, judge Haas. Her next project is considered a minor *film noir*. *The Other Woman* (1954) tells the story

of a struggling starlet who blackmails a wealthy producer (Haas). Claiming she carries his child, she demands $50,000. He kills her and almost gets away with it. Although the Haas/Moore movies consistently received poor reviews, they proved to be money makers anyway. Because of the profit these movies made, Columbia signed Cleo as a contract player. They had her take the route every rising starlet in Hollywood had to go: posing for the pin-up photographers and

WITH JACK INGRAM AND DON MCGUIRE IN *CONGO BILL*, 1948 (COLUMBIA).

making publicity appearances. She was molded as a sexy blonde in the Monroe tradition. Cleo was unhappy with this, and once commented: "When you're a blonde and mother nature has been good to you, you have a chance in the movie business. But the biggest problem is that producers still think that blondes can't act. Since someone came up with the tag 'dumb blonde,' the whole of America seems convinced that the lot of us actresses are dumb broads." At this stage of her career, Cleo still lived with her family (her parents and a younger brother and sister) in the town of Tarzana, about 20 miles from Hollywood. For a while she was romantically linked to singer Vic Damone, actor Dan Dailey, baseball player Joe DiMaggio and singer Tony Travis. Cleo's career was progressing nicely. She was named one of the top most promising actresses of 1954. But, then, Columbia chief Harry Cohn had decided that their new blonde starlet, Kim Novak, was to be the blonde to compete with 20th Century-Fox star Marilyn Monroe; so Cleo lost the starring role in the film *Pushover* (1954) to Kim Novak. Cleo had

WITH DAVID BRIAN IN *THE GREAT JEWEL ROBBER*, 1949 (WARNER BROS.)

WITH VICTOR MATURE IN *GAMBLING HOUSE*, 1951 (RKO).

just finished another movie with Hugo Haas. *Bait* (1954) was much publicized for Cleo's (then) daring bathtub scene. When she was in Chicago for promotional purposes, she was interviewed by Jack Eigen for his television show. At one moment during this interview the talk got around to movie censorship and the imposed limits on film kisses. Eigen then suggested that he and Cleo go for the record over live TV. This resulted in the famous five-minute kiss. After the

ONE GIRL'S CONFESSION, 1953 (COLUMBIA).

show, hundreds of complaints came in from viewers and the story made front pages around the country. Cleo successfully exploited the incident for months. The year was rounded out by a television appearance on *The Ford Television Theatre*, in an episode called "Remember to Live." Cleo played Lana, one of Korean war veteran Dane Clark's girlfriends. As to be expected, Dane eventually chose the other girl — Barbara Hale - to "go steady." As the old saying goes, "Gentlemen prefer blondes, but they marry brunettes!" The show was aired by NBC on November 4. To promote her next movie, *Hold Back Tomorrow* (1955), Cleo toured 66 cities with co-star John Agar. The film critics gave Cleo some good reviews. "When I played a scene with apparently dark — because soaking wet - hair in *Hold Back Tomorrow*, critics really noticed me. They called me an actress of rare talent! It seems to me this is something that can't depend on the color of my hair?!" Columbia starred Cleo in two minor A-programmers under the direction of director Lewis Seiler. She got a part in his *Women's Prison* (1955)

OVER-EXPOSED, 1956 (COLUMBIA).

WITH VINCE EDWARDS IN *HIT AND RUN,* 1957 (UNITED ARTISTS).

with Ida Lupino and Jan Sterling. Today, this is a cult classic and it certainly is Cleo's most famous film. The next project was said to be especially written for her. In *Over-Exposed* (1956), she played once model, now photographer Lila Crane who finds herself in trouble with the mob, because she shot some compromising photos. Her gowns were especially designed for her by fashion designer Jean-Louis. England's *Picturegoer* magazine wrote about Cleo's acting: "Buxom Cleo Moore makes the best of a sketchy part." Because the old studio system was dying all around in the late 1950s, Cleo's contract at Columbia wasn't prolonged. Her last film was again a Hugo Haas production. In *Hit and Run* (1957), she played the cheating wife of garage owner Haas who romances his employee Vince Edwards. Together they plan to get rid of Haas. The film was distributed by United Artists. Cleo moved out of her family's home in 1958. With no other film offers coming, Cleo enrolled at UCLA for a course in law and psychology. More and more she shrugged off the dumb blonde qualification she disliked so much. "A blonde has to be a lot smarter than a brunette… because she has to go through life proving how dumb she isn't." She was also still active in the construction business. In the mid-fifties Cleo had started a building construction enterprise with her father. On November 19, 1961, Cleo married Herb Heftler. She became a mother when in 1963 she gave birth to their daughter. Cleo Moore died on October 25, 1973, in Inglewood, California, from a heart attack.

CLEO MOORE FILMOGRAPHY

1948: *Embraceable You* (blonde), *Congo Bill* (Lureen/Ruth Culver).
1950: *Bright Leaf* (Cousin Louise), *This Side of the Law, 711 Ocean Drive* (Hal's date), *The Great Jewel Robbery* (blonde date), *Dynamite Pass* (Lulu), *Rio Grande Patrol* (Peppie), *Hunt the Man Down* (Pat Sheldon).
1951: *Gambling House* (Sally).
1952: *The Pace That Thrills* (Ruby), *On Dangerous Ground* (Myrna Bowers), *Strange Fascination* (Margo).
1953: *One Girl's Confession* (Mary Adams), *Thy Neighbor's Wife* (Lita Vojnar, the judge's wife).
1954: *Bait* (Peggy), *The Other Woman* (Sherry Steward).
1955: *Hold Back Tomorrow* (Dora), *Women's Prison* (Mae).
1956: *Over-Exposed* (Lila Crane/Lily Krenska).
1957: *Hit and Run* (Susie Hilmer).

Barbara Nichols

Barbara Nichols was born Barbara Marie Nickerauer in Mineola, New York, on December 30, 1929. Her parents, George and Julia, decided to move to Jamaica when their only child was in her early teens. There, Barbara attended Woodrow Wilson High School. She won many beauty contests while still at school and after graduation appeared in a hotel floor show in Ciudad Trujillo, Dominican Republic for two months. In the late forties she returned to the US, began to model and was a burlesque dancer before she appeared on television and stage in the early fifties. Barbara replaced television personality Dagmar on TV's *Broadway Open House* in 1951. Her picture in *Esquire* magazine led to the part of Valerie in *Pal Joey* (January 3, 1952-April 18, 1953) on Broadway.

BEYOND A REASONABLE DOUBT, 1956 (RKO).

In this period of her life, Barbara decided to get a nose job, to remove the little lump on her nose. She did a lot of television shows, when Hollywood finally took notice of this vivacious blonde and she made her debut in Marilyn Monroe's *River of No Return* (1954), as a dancer in the saloon scenes. In 1955, she dated actor Steve Cochran, whom she had a recurring relationship with until 1958. (Cochran apparently had a thing for blonde starlets; he also dated Jayne

WITH JANET LEIGH AND JOI LANSING IN *WHO WAS THAT LADY?*, 1960 (COLUMBIA).

Mansfield in 1955 and was the steady beau of British glamour star Sabrina in the late fifties.) Barbara had no problems finding new television and film roles, and found herself busy stealing the spotlight in small, wisecracking roles. Mostly cast as strippers, gold-diggers, gun molls and other floozy types named Lola, Dolly, Birdie or Poopsie, Barbara made the best of her roles. Clark Gable was her co-star in *The King and Four Queens* (1956) and she had a key role in RKO's *Beyond a Reasonable Doubt* (1956) as Dolly Moore who provided an alibi for murder suspect Dana Andrews. In 1957 she got some nice roles in good films. She was seen as the wisecracking co-worker of Doris Day in *The Pajama Game* and played a sharp-tongued showgirl colleague of Kim Novak in *Pal Joey*. Since Kim Novak and Barbara had the same shade of blonde hair, it was suggested that Barbara changed hers to a brassier hue. It is said that because of this, the two actresses didn't speak off-camera for the duration of filming. Maybe her best part that

THE LOVED ONE, 1965 (MGM).

year was that of vulnerable cigarette girl Rita in *Sweet Smell of Success*. The critics were very enthusiastic about the movie and Barbara landed some good reviews, too. She had a couple of good scenes with Tony Curtis, playing her "boyfriend" who is willing to share his girl for a raise on the ladder of success. Even though Barbara makes clear she is not "that sort of girl," Curtis talks her into spending the night with a man she hardly knows. Although she was not considered star

WITH GARY COOPER IN *TEN NORTH FREDERICK*, 1958 (20TH CENTURY FOX).

material by Hollywood producers, Barbara was much in demand for co-starring roles the following years. A nice part — earning her $ 1,000 for one day of work — opposite Gary Cooper (in the dress Marilyn Monroe wore in *The Seven Year Itch*) in *Ten North Frederick* (1958) and a part as the unfaithful wife of soldier Aldo Ray in *The Naked and the Dead* (1958), earned her the name "The Brooklyn Monroe." When Ray returns home from the front, he finds Barbara hastily putting on a dressing gown. As he bursts in on her lover, she yells, "Sam, don't hit him. He's from the finance company!" By the end of the decade her film career had hit the skids and she turned more and more to TV, guest starring on *The Bob Cummings Show* (in an episode called "Bob and the Dumb Blonde," 1958) and as a stripper on *The Untouchables* (1959). Her *Untouchables* episodes were later put together and released as the motion picture *The Scarface Mob* (1962) in Europe. Barbara landed only one regular role, in the very short-lived sitcom *Love that Jill* (1958), in which she played a model named Ginger. Barbara must

THE PAJAMA GAME, 1957 (WARNER BROS.).

be the only blonde in this book who wore the most of Marilyn Monroe's film costumes in her movies; in a scene from *Woman Obsessed* (1959), she was seen in the red button-down dress Marilyn wore in *Niagara* (1953). The Columbia comedy, *Who Was That Lady* (1960) reunited her with fellow blonde Joi Lansing. Back in 1953, when they both were modeling for Bernard of Hollywood, they were invited to have dinner with Clark Gable and the photographer. In *Who*

WITH TONY CURTIS IN *SWEET SMELL OF SUCCESS*, 1957 (UNITED ARTISTS).

Was That Lady?, the pair of them played the sexy Coogle sisters. Another blonde team-up came with *The George Raft Story* (1961) for Allied Artists, with Jayne Mansfield and Ray Danton. Barbara played entertainer Texas Guinan, dressed in Monroe's *Some Like it Hot* dress, greeting her audience with the raucous cry of "Hello, suckers, how's the mob treating you?" before giving a sing and dance show (in her own voice; she had earlier been dubbed while singing in *Where the*

Boys Are [1960] for MGM). In 1961, she starred in an unsold pilot for a proposed sitcom about airline hostesses called *Coffee, Tea or Milk*. The CBS television network later broadcasted the pilot on their *Vacation Playhouse* program. The new title was *All About Barbara*. It aired on August 16, 1963. She was back on Broadway when she starred with George Gobel and Sam Levene in the musical *Let It Ride* in 1961 (October 12-December 9). Together with Mamie Van Doren and

WITH JIM HUTTON IN *LOOKING FOR LOVE*, 1964 (MGM).

Angie Dickinson, she appeared on TV show *The Dick Powell Theatre* (1962). In the episode "No Strings Attached," Dick Powell is a lawyer who has to decide between his high-class girlfriend (Angie) and the burlesque stripper client he's just acquired (Mamie Van Doren). Mamie is upset that rival Barbara Nichols has stolen her act...which consists of dressing up like a sexy missile and with each hip swivel, firing off explosive blasts! Back in the Hollywood film studios she played in a variety of roles. Although her part in *The World of Henry Orient* (1963) ended up on the cutting room floor, she was seen in the prison drama *House of Women* (1962), had a part in the Glenn Ford comedy *Dear Heart* (1964) and had a starring role in the mediocre sci-fi flick *The Human Duplicators* (1965), starring George Nader and Richard Kiel. Unlike Jayne Mansfield, Barbara's part wasn't cut out of the all-star black comedy *The Loved One* (1965). After small parts in the Ann-Margret movie, *The Swinger* (1966), and the science-fiction film *The Power* (1968), with George Hamilton and Suzanne Pleshette, Barbara quit acting for a while. She did appear on television occasionally. By the mid-'70s Barbara had developed a life-threatening liver disease. Her health deteriorated rapidly and she died on October 5, 1976 at the age of 46.

BARBARA NICHOLS FILMOGRAPHY

1954: *River of No Return* (dancer).

1956: *Manfish* (Mimi), *Miracle in the Rain* (Arlene Witchy), *Beyond a Reasonable Doubt* (Dolly Moore), *The King and Four Queens* (Birdie McDade), *The Wild Party* (Sandy).

1957: *Sweet Smell of Success* (Rita), *The Pajama Game* (Poopsie), *Pal Joey* (Gladys).

1958: *The Naked and the Dead* (Mildred), *Ten North Frederick* (Stella).

1959: *Woman Obsessed* (Mayme Radzevitch), *That Kind of Woman* (Jane).

1960: *Who Was That Lady?* (Gloria Coogle), *Where the Boys Are* (Lola Fandango).

1961: *The George Raft Story* (Texas Guinan).

1962: *The Scarface Mob* (Brandy La France), *House of Women* (Candy Kane).

1964: *The World of Henry Orient*, *Dear Heart* (June Loveland), *The Disorderly Orderly* (Miss Marlowe), *Looking for Love* (Gaye Swinger).

1965: *The Loved One* (Sadie Blodgett), *The Human Duplicators* (Gale Wilson).

1966: *The Swinger* (Blossom La Tour).

1968: *The Power* (Flora), *Sette Uomini e un cervello/Criminal Affair*.

1973: *Charley and the Angel* (Sadie).

1975: *The Photographer* (Mrs. Wilde).

1976: *Won Ton Ton, the Dog Who Saved Hollywood* (Nick's girl).

20th CENTURY FOX

Sheree North

Sheree North was born Dawn Shirley Bethel, in Hollywood, January 17, 1933. Together with her half-brother Don and her half-sister Janet, she was raised by her mother and grandmother, because shortly after she was born her mother, June Shoard, and father, Edward Bethel, divorced. "I was born in the heart of Hollywood, but I don't remember the house because our family moved right after that. I don't remember my father either. I never knew him. He left my mother before I was born, and she never talked about him." (In 1957 Sheree discovered that Edward Bethel had been her stepfather. Her real father, Richard Francis Crang, died in late 1956.) When she was ten, Sheree added five years to her age and began dancing at the U.S.O. When she was thirteen, she became part of the company at the open air Greek Theatre in Hollywood's Griffith Park. "I had to dress up and lie about my age. I was well developed and it wasn't hard to do." It was

WITH JERRY LEWIS IN *LIVING IT UP!*, 1954 (PARAMOUNT).

WITH BETTY GRABLE, ORSON BEAN AND BOB CUMMINGS IN *HOW TO BE VERY, VERY POPULAR*, 1955 (20TH CENTURY FOX).

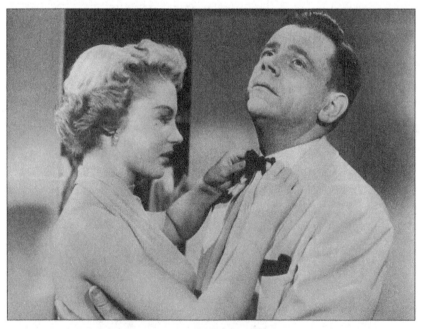

WITH TOM EWELL IN *THE LIEUTENANT WORE SKIRTS*, 1956 (20TH CENTURY FOX).

at this point in her career that she adopted her professional name. She worked at the Greek Theatre for three summers. At age fifteen she married Fred Bessire who was ten years her senior. The next year she gave birth to her daughter, Dawn. The marriage to Bessire lasted eighteen months, but the official divorce came in 1952. Being a single mother, she made a living for her daughter and herself dancing in nightclubs. She also tried modeling and had a few bit parts in Hollywood

movies. By this time Sheree had dyed her hair platinum blonde. In the meantime, Sheree's daughter was growing up and beginning to miss her mother when she was away dancing. Sheree decided to become a secretary so she could spend more time with her daughter. Just around that time, dance director Bob Alton was searching for dancers for an upcoming Broadway show. He asked Sheree, but she declined several times. Finally, she decided to do the show, and left for New York. For her appearance in the Broadway musical *Hazel Flagg* (1953) as a sexy jitterbug dancer, she won the 1953 Theatre World Award. The show opened on Broadway on February 11, 1953. Sheree became an immediate sensation, and was proclaimed "Broadway's answer to Marilyn Monroe." Her role led to a part in the film version, *Living it Up!* (1954) at Paramount, and soon thereafter 20th Century-Fox signed her to a contract. Because Fox's main attraction, Marilyn Monroe, refused to play the sexy dumb blonde roles offered, Fox threatened to give these roles to Sheree North. Monroe took the role in *There's No Business Like Show Business* (1954), but refused to do *How to be Very, Very Popular* (1955). Thus, the part went to Sheree. Sheree and Betty Grable played a couple of nightclub workers who witness a murder and hide out at a men's college. The highlight of this mediocre movie was Sheree's "Shake, Rattle and Roll" number. British *Picturegoer* wrote in their review: "Why, oh why, cast this blonde with so much bubble in a role that calls on her to be hypnotized by a student in the first twenty minutes and then sleepwalk her way through the rest of the film?" In 1955 she married music publisher John Freeman in Arizona. She made a few other movies at Fox, when in 1956 they hired the talents of Jayne Mansfield to keep their blonde

WITH JEFFREY HUNTER IN *THE WAY TO THE GOLD*, 1957 (20TH CENTURY FOX).

queen Marilyn in place. Sheree told the press at that time, "Jayne's much better equipped than I am to compete with Marilyn." While Jayne was hired to star in comedy musical *The Girl Can't Help It*, Sheree got a starring role in the classy musical *The Best Things in Life are Free* (1956). Sheree played the love interest of Gordon MacRae. She has a sensational dance number called 'The Birth of the Blues." *Picturegoer* said of her performance, "…and Sheree North brings a surprising warmth and sympathy to her role." In 1957 she played a straight role in *Way to the Gold* (1957), which was received positively by the press. "Let's face it, these blonde bombshells quickly become bores. That's why I'm double glad that my favourite b.b. Sheree North, has eased out of the glamour groove. Sheree North is touchingly funny as the pinch-penny skivvy with a cash-register brain." (*Picturegoer*, July 6 1957). That same year she divorced John Freeman. Sheree's blonde hair was dyed back to her natural brown, and in 1958 she quit the film business for a while. (20th Century-Fox did use a blonde pin-up pose of Sheree to decorate a bedroom wall in *Fraulein*, 1958.) On December 17, 1958, she married her psychiatrist, Dr. Gerhardt Sommer. Her second daughter, Erica, was born a year later. In the early sixties she appeared on the stage in *Thursday is a Good Night*, with former *The Lieutenant Wore Skirts* co-star Tom Ewell, divorced Sommer, accepted some television offers and returned to Hollywood to star in *Destination Inner Space* (1966). Besides appearing in movies, she also continued to work in the theatre. In 1971 she co-starred opposite Burt Lancaster in the western *Lawman* (1971). As an ex-hooker and old girlfriend of Lancaster, the movie marked her first nude scenes. In 1980, Sheree played in a biographical TV movie about the woman she was compared to early in her career. She played the small part of Marilyn Monroe's mother in *Marilyn: The Untold Story*. Sheree North, who once started out as a nightclub showgirl, took the route of a Monroe impersonator to character actress; and achieved praise and respect in the movie and television business over the years. She sadly passed away on November 4, 2005 (age 72) after complications from cancer surgery, leaving her fourth husband, Philip Norman, and her two daughters behind.

SHEREE NORTH FILMOGRAPHY

1950: *Force of Arms.*
1951: *Excuse My Dust* (club member).
1952: *The Jazz Singer.*
1953: *Here Come the Girls* (blonde harem/showgirl).
1954: *Living it Up!* (herself, jitterbug dancer).
1955: *How to be Very Very Popular* (Curly).
1956: *The Lieutenant Wore Skirts* (Kathy Whitcomb), *The Best Things in Life are Free* (Kitty).
1957: *The Way to the Gold* (Hank Clifford*)*, *No Down Payment* (Isabelle Flagg).
1958: *In Love and War* (Lorraine), *Mardi Gras* (Eadie).
1966: *Destination Inner Space* (Sandra).
1968: *Madigan* (Jonesy).
1969: *The Trouble with Girls* (Nita Bix), *The Gypsy Moths* (waitress), Survival (Sheree).
1971: *The Lawman* (Laura Selby), *The Organization* (Mrs. Gloria Morgan).
1973: *Charley Varrick* (Jewell Everett), *The Outfit* (Buck's wife).
1975: *Breakout* (Myrna).
1976: *The Shootist* (Serepta).
1977: *Telefon* (Marie Wills).
1978: *Rabbit Test* (mystery woman).
1979: *Only Once in a Lifetime* (Sally).
1988: *Maniac Cop* (Sally Noland).
1990: *Cold Dog Soup* (Mrs. Hughes).
1991: *Defenseless* (Mrs. Bodeck).
1998: *Susan's Plan* (Mrs. Beyers).

Kim Novak

In 1954 Kim Novak was a beginning starlet at Columbia. But by the end of the following year she already was second to Marilyn Monroe as the public's favorite actress at the box office. Beautiful hazel-eyed Kim had become the new sensation of the press. She was seen on different magazine covers, was profiled in many articles and was considered the actress to take over the throne of reigning Columbia queen Rita Hayworth. Director Richard Quine once said of her, "She had the proverbial quality of the lady in the parlour and the whore in the bedroom. Kim has a ladylike quality, but it goes a step further. She had a combination of that with sex appeal and a childlike quality." Kim Novak was born Marilyn Pauline Novak, in Chicago, on February 13, 1933. She attended public schools in Chicago and was said to be an indifferent student. She was shy, withdrawn, tall for her age and thin. Feeling that her daughter needed training as a

model to give her the confidence she lacked, her mother, Blanche, induced her to join a group called the Fair Teens Club. Appearing much more mature than her real age, she embarked on a professional modeling career when she was only eleven. After graduation from Farragut High School, she spent a year and a half at Wright Junior College. There she majored in drama, but only succeeded in getting a part in one play, *Our Town*. During the summer vacation Kim was chosen to tour New York, Georgia, Texas and California for a washing machine and refrigerator company. The tour ended in San Francisco, but Kim

WITH FRED MACMURRAY IN *PUSHOVER*, 1954 (COLUMBIA).

and a girlfriend went on to Los Angeles. She went to the Caroline Leonetti Modeling Agency and eventually found herself hired as one of the fifteen models to appear in the film *The French Line* (1954) at RKO. (The movie was actually filmed in 1953, but, due to censorship problems, it was shelved for a year. The same thing happened to Kim's other RKO movie, *Son of Sinbad*.) When Columbia boss Harry Cohn was searching for a young new face to replace studio star

WITH FRANK SINATRA IN *THE MAN WITH THE GOLDEN ARM*, 1955 (UNITED ARTISTS).

Rita Hayworth he was persuaded by casting director Max Arnow to give Kim a chance. Cohn didn't take much of a liking to her, but agreed to sign her to a contract. Her first role at Columbia was well received by the press. In *Pushover* (1954) she played the feminine lead next to Fred MacMurray and Phil Carey. The public also took a liking to Kim and she was soon offered more film roles. Cohn began realizing that his "fat Polack" (as he called her behind her back), was the promising glamour star he needed to compete with Fox's hot star Monroe and that she was the girl to become the top-grossing moneymaker at his studio. Columbia cancelled plans to borrow Sheree North to play "the other woman," and Kim was cast in a Monroe-ish part as the dumb but friendly blonde, in the comedy *Phffft!* (1955). Her co-stars were Jack Lemmon and blonde Judy Holliday. She starts the film with a demonstration of how to pronounce the title — the sound of a marriage breaking up — in a voice evidently based on Marilyn Monroe.

WITH JUDY HOLIDAY AND JACK LEMMON IN *PHFFFT!*, 1954 (COLUMBIA).

Kim's third film assignment from Columbia was a suspenseful melodrama called *5 Against the House* (1955). The role required Kim to sing two songs in her portrayal of a nightclub singer. Although she took singing lessons and Columbia's publicity department stated that it was Kim's voice we heard on the soundtrack, singer Jo Ann Greer dubbed the two numbers in the final film version. In *The Man with the Golden Arm* (1955) she gave a strong performance as the girl in the

WITH CANTIFLAS IN *PEPE*, 1960 (COLUMBIA).

flat downstairs who helps Frank Sinatra kick his drug habit by locking him in her apartment. British *Picturegoer* magazine said of Kim: "She adds a new dimension to that classic film cliché, the good-hearted tramp." In *Picnic* (1955) she played a wistful country girl (Kim Stanley's stage part) seduced by William Holden. Both films were big successes. In 1956, Kim's cinema popularity reached an all-time high. Kim was named by *Box-Office* magazine as one of the ten most popular movie stars. She was rushed into one film after the other. For her part, in *The Eddy Duchin Story* (1956), with Tyrone Power, she received some good reviews. *Picturegoer* wrote: "Kim Novak proves her worth again: there's a womanliness about the girl that is so much more than mere sex appeal." When asked about her career rise at that time, she answered, "I've always had to work hard. Once I worked an elevator when funds were low. I've had a job as receptionist to a dentist assistant. I had no ambition as an actress until that day when Columbia signed me to a contract. I didn't even go to the movies much before I started

VERTIGO, 1958 (PARAMOUNT).

to work in Hollywood." Her lack of ambition was sometimes seen in her movie performances. In *Pal Joey* (1957), with Rita Hayworth and Frank Sinatra, the press accused her of looking bored and disinterested in her role. *Photoplay* (March 1958) considered her career over: "She has no personality beyond a publicity handout, and has outstripped her meagre talent." The audience, however, cherished its dreamy, vulnerable star, and in 1958 Alfred Hitchcock asked her to play

WITH TONY RANDALL IN *BOYS' NIGHT OUT*, 1962 (MGM).

a role in his *Vertigo*. (Kim was actually his second choice, since Vera Miles was unavailable.) In this movie her solemn and detached acting were needed in her role of Madeleine Elster, the mysterious blonde who fascinates ex-detective James Stewart. Again with Stewart, she played a witch in *Bell, Book and Candle* (1958) and a year later she starred with Fredric March in the drama *Middle of the Night*. She gave a good performance as a youngster attracted to an older man, but the film wasn't a success. Still, the movie was selected as the United States entry at the 1959 Cannes Film Festival. Kim was officially chosen to represent Columbia Pictures, and so she left for a thirty-day tour through Europe. The next year, Kim was entirely convincing in her best film for director Richard Quine (*Pushover, Bell, Book and Candle* and *The Notorious Landlady* were the others), *Strangers When We Meet* (1960). There she has a husband (John Bryant) whom she can't arouse to any sexual response and gets into an affair with Kirk Douglas. During the sixties, Kim Novak only played in a few movies. For MGM she did a comedy, *Boys' Night Out* (1962), as a sociologist studying extramarital activity. Although Kim proved in this picture that she was a creditable comedienne, the press thought different. *The New York Times* wrote: "But then it must be said that Kim Novak is not a glowing inspiration as the girl. Her inclination to ardor appears no more powerful than her passion for a doctor's degree." For Columbia she had

WITH RAY WALSTON IN *KISS ME, STUPID*, 1964 (UNITED ARTISTS).

already filmed another comedy, *The Notorious Landlady* (1962), which was released after *Boys' Night Out*. Also in 1962, 20th Century-Fox offered her Marilyn Monroe's role in *Something's Got to Give*, after they had fired Monroe. Kim declined. When she learned that Monroe passed away just a few months later, she commented: "With Marilyn it's so sad because she didn't have a family, really. I think you need roots. You certainly don't get them in this business." Columbia released her from her contract and Kim took a year off to enjoy the countryside and peace of the house she had bought after the completion of *The Notorious Landlady*. Then she was cast as the Cockney waitress in the remake of *Of Human Bondage* (1964). The critics roasted her and co-star Laurence Harvey, and the film died the death. So did *Kiss Me, Stupid* (1964), but mainly because director Billy Wilder was attacked for bad taste and many exhibitors refused to play it. Kim played Polly the Pistol, the star attraction among the cocktail waitresses at the Belly Button Café, placed in a town called Climax, Nevada. These days, the film isn't that raunchy anymore. Kim actually plays a good role as the sensitive waitress/prostitute.

At the time of its release the press was divided by negative and more positive reviews. *Films and Filming* wrote: "As the tart with a gentle heart, Kim Novak's performance is her familiar one, but as touching as ever. Here is a part Marilyn might have played, and the comparison underlines how, where the screen Marilyn was only a performer, a comedienne, Kim's slower, heavier style is essentially a tragedienne's." While filming *The Amorous Adventures of Moll Flanders* (1965)

WITH RICHARD JOHNSON IN *THE AMOROUS ADVENTURES OF MOLL FLANDERS*, 1965 (PARAMOUNT).

in London, she fell in love and married her co-star, Richard Johnson, on March 15, 1965. (Their marriage only lasted a year; the couple divorced on May 26 1966.) After a three-year absence from the screen, Kim Novak returned for director Robert Aldrich's *The Legend of Lylah Clare* (1968). In it she played a dual role of an actress who is to portray a once famous actress in a movie biography. Kim did a fine job in the film and never looked more beautiful. The part, the playing of two characters within the same personality, was reminiscent of her role in *Vertigo*. The movie was a commercial bust. When actress Melina Mercouri wasn't available for *The Great Bank Robbery* (1969), Warner Bros. negotiated for Kim to star

THE LEGEND OF LYLAH CLARE, 1968 (MGM).

in this Western-comedy. Kim quit acting for a while. In the seventies she appeared on television and made several movies. She fell in love with her veterinarian, Robert Malloy, and married him on March 12, 1976. In the seventies and eighties she made some movies and appeared on television, but the remainder of her life has been dividing her time between her animals and painting. When asked about her ambitions in 1956, she answered: "My ambition? A small ranch house, with a small horse to ride." Maybe her down to earth-ness made her one of the few blondes who survived the media and publicity craze in their heyday and their career decline in the late sixties.

KIM NOVAK FILMOGRAPHY

1954: *The French Line* (model on stairs), *Pushover* (Lona McLane), *Phffft!* (Janis).

1955: *Son of Sinbad* (Raider), *5 Against the House* (Kay Greylek), *Picnic* (Madge Ownes), *The Man with the Golden Arm* (Molly).

1956: *The Eddy Duchin Story* (Marjorie Oelrichs Duchin).

1957: *Jeanne Eagels* (Jeanne Eagels), *Pal Joey* (Linda English).

1958: *Vertigo* (Madeleine Elster/Judy Barton), *Bell, Book and Candle* (Gillian Holroyd).

1959: *Middle of the Night* (Betty Preisser).

1960: *Strangers When We Meet* (Maggie Gault), *Pepe* (herself, cameo appearance).

1962: *The Notorious Landlady* (Carlyle Hardwicke), *Boys' Night Out* (Cathy).

1964: *Of Human Bondage* (Mildred Rogers), *Kiss Me, Stupid* (Polly the Pistol/Zelda).

1965: *The Amorous Adventures of Moll Flanders* (Moll Flanders).

1968: *The Legend of Lylah Clare* (Elsa Brinkmann/Lylah Clare).

1969: *The Great Bank Robbery* (Lyda Kebanov).

1973: *Tales That Witness Madness* (Auriol Pageant).

1977: *The White Buffalo* (Mrs. "Poker" Jenny Schermerhorn).

1979: *Schöner Gigolo, Armer Gigolo/Just a Gigolo* (Helga).

1980: *The Mirror Crack'd* (Lola Brewster).

1987: *Es hat mich Sehr Gefreut*.

1990: *The Children* (Rose Sellars).

1991: *Liebestraum* (Lillian Anderson Munnsen).

Gloria Pall

Considered too hot for television, Gloria's sexy TV personality Voluptua (who, negligee clad, presented late night movies from her parlour) only lasted seven weeks before she was taken off the air, because of dozens of complaints from angry viewers. Gloria stated in a *Modern Man* magazine article, "The funny things about my Voluptua program in my seven weeks on the air was that I got more requests for pinups than letters of criticism." Gloria Pall has written a couple of books about her Hollywood days and still knows how to promote herself these days as a glamorous pin-up queen from the fifties. She was born July 15, 1927, in Brooklyn, New York. After winning the "Miss Flatbush" beauty competition, Gloria started to model (including nude modeling) and eventually became a showgirl in Las Vegas. Gloria arrived in Hollywood

THE CRIMSON KIMONO, 1959 (COLUMBIA).

WITH PERCY KILBRIDE IN *MA AND PA KETTLE ON VACATION*, 1953 (UNIVERSAL).

WITH MARILYN HANOLD IN *THE GARMENT JUNGLE*, 1957 (COLUMBIA).

in 1952. Standing 5 foot and 9 inches made it not easy finding good movie parts. When she was invited to Ray Anthony's party for Marilyn Monroe to announce the song "Mmm…Marilyn," she showed up in a very low-cut dress and almost stole all attention from the guest of honor. Her first claim to movie fame was when she appeared as Valupta in the serial *Commando Cody* (1953). She did a lot of television before Universal took her in for some small roles in *All Ashore, Ma and Pa Kettle on Vacation* and *Abbott and Costello Go to Mars* in 1953. After two featured parts on television in *Where's Raymond?*, with Ray Bolger ,and *Space Patrol* (both 1954) and her stint as Voluptua, she landed a featured part in Republic's *City of Shadows* (1955). Unfortunately for Gloria, it was back to bit parts and in December 1955 she left for a USO Christmas tour in Europe. She also went to England, where she discussed a Voluptua show with the BBC (which was never realized) and had a walk-on appearance in a show called *On the Town*, with Ron Randell. Back in the United States she married actor Robert Eaton and divorced him a year later, because he was cheating on her. Her agent landed her two roles at MGM. The first one was Elvis Presley's *Jailhouse Rock* (1957). In the movie she was a stripper, but only her legs were seen. Her second film at MGM was *The Brothers Karamazov* (1958). She's the girl in the opening scene of the film held by two men and tickled with a feather under her feet. A bigger part was that of stripper Sugar Torch in Columbia's *The Crimson Kimono* (1959). After that it was back to small parts in films and on television for Gloria. In 1964 she married (to auto dealer Allen Kane) again and departed from showbiz.

GLORIA PALL FILMOGRAPHY

1952: *Actors and Sin.*

1953: *Paris Model* (mannequin), *Marry Me Again, All Ashore* (Lucretia), *Ma and Pa Kettle on Vacation* (French girl with poodle), *Abbott and Costello Go to Mars* (tall girl in New York).

1954: *20,000 Leagues Under the Sea* (girlfriend), *The French Line* (showgirl).

1955: *Night of the Hunter* (saloon girl), *Son of Sinbad* (harem raider), *City of Shadows* (Voluptua, waitress).

1956: *Hot Shots* (girl at party).

1957: *The Wrong Man, This Could Be the Night* (new girl), *Jailhouse Rock* (stripper), *The Garment Jungle* (fitting model).

1958: *The Brothers Karamazov* (girl being tickled).

1959: *The Crimson Kimono* (Sugar Torch, stripper).

1960: *Elmer Gantry* (gal in brothel).

1961: *Ada* (party guest).

Dorothy Provine

Although Dorothy Provine's career peaked in the sixties, she played some great parts in grade-B teenage movies in the fifties. Her appearance in those movies secured her a part in this book. She was born on January 20, 1937, in Deadwood, South Dakota. After she graduated from the University of Washington with a degree in Theatre Arts, she went to Hollywood and started out in the title role of *The Bonnie Parker Story* (1958), for AIP. Immediately from the movie's opening scene, Dorothy Provine makes a strong impression as Roaring Twenties gangster Bonnie Parker. The movie is entertaining and well-acted. She played in some other movies, before finding real fame on television as Pinky Pinkham, the Charleston-dancing flapper in the Warner Bros. adventure series *The Roaring 20's* (1960). In 1963 she played a good part in *Wall of Noise*, in which she was Ty Hardin's girl, faithful to him even when he is getting involved with another woman. Some funny comedies like *Good Neighbor Sam* (1964), with Jack Lemmon, and *The Great Race* (1965), with Lemmon and Tony Curtis, followed. In 1968 she married English-born director Robert Day and quit acting a year later. (In the seventies she sporadically showed up on television.)

DOROTHY PROVINE FILMOGRAPHY

1958: *The Bonnie Parker Story* (Bonnie Parker), *Live Fast, Die Young* (Jackie).
1959: *Riot in Juvenile Prison* (Babe), *The 30 Foot Bride of Candy Rock* (Emmy Lou Raven).
1963: *Wall of Noise* (Ann Conroy), *It's a Mad Mad Mad Mad World* (Emeline Marcus-Finch).
1964: *Good Neighbor Sam* (Minerva Bissel).
1965: *The Great Race* (Lily Olay), *That Darn Cat!* (Ingrid Randall).
1966: *Se tutte le Donne del Mondo/Kiss the Girls and Make Them Die* (Susan Fleming).
1967: *Who's Minding the Mint?* (Verna Baxter).
1968: *Never a Dull Moment* (Sally Inwood).

THE 30 FOOT BRIDE OF CANDY ROCK, 1959 (COLUMBIA).

THE BONNIE PARKER STORY, 1958 (AIP).

WITH NORMA EBERHARDT IN *LIVE FAST, DIE YOUNG*, 1958 (UNIVERSAL).

Juli Reding

Voluptuous Juli Reding was better known for her pin-up layouts in men's magazines like *Fling, Scamp* and *Snap* then for her movie roles. Nevertheless, she managed to appear in a movie that is now somewhat famous by connoisseurs of the mediocre: *Tormented* (1960). In this movie she plays the ex-girlfriend of Richard Carlson, who accidentally falls to her death and returns as a ghost to haunt Carlson. Juli Reding was born in Quanah, Texas, on November 28, 1935. Her birth name is Esther Fay Reding. She arrived in Hollywood in 1956 and winning a beauty contest got her signed by Warner Bros. She was cast in a recurring role in the Red Skelton show on television and played small parts at Warners. Warners changed her then-stage name of Julie Otis to Juli Reding. With roommate and friend Sandra Giles she was seen all over town during those days. Her press agent Sheldon Davis was handling PR for the opening of the Fremont Hotel in Las Vegas and needed a good-looking gal for a stunt. He first offered it to Juli, who worked as a receptionist in an adjoining office. Because she'd just been picked to be one of the Mermaids at Marineland, she suggested her friend Sandra Giles to Davis. After a couple of small movie parts (as Julie Reding), she starred in *Mission in Morocco* (1959) with Lex Barker. In the early sixties she finally landed herself some meatier roles in *Tormented* and *Why Must I Die?* (both 1960). She married Mari Blanchard's ex-husband, Reese Taylor, in 1962, and was Rita Marlowe in the Los Angeles

VICE RAID, 1959 (UNITED ARTISTS).

WITH RICHARD CARLSON IN *TORMENTED*, 1960 (ALLIED ARTISTS).

theatres in the play *Will Success Spoil Rock Hunter?* the next year. She divorced Taylor in 1964 and married Zsa Zsa Gabor's ex-husband, Herb Hutner, in 1969. That same year she ended her showbiz career.

WHY MUST I DIE?, 1960 (AIP).

JULI REDING FILMOGRAPHY

1957: *The Helen Morgan Story* (cigarette girl).
1958: *Cowboy* (girlfriend), *Darby's Rangers* (sexy girl).
1959: *Vice Raid* (Gertie), *Mission in Morocco* (Carol Sampson).
1960: *Why Must I Die?* (Mitzi), *Tormented* (Vi Mason).
1962: *The Interns* (Party Girl).

SATAN IN HIGH HEELS, 1962 (COSMIC FILMS INC.)

Sabrina

Norma Ann Sykes was born on May 19, 1936, in Stockport, UK. At the age of twelve she was struck by polio and was hospitalized for two years. Sabrina and her family moved to Blackpool in 1949, which she left that same year to search for fame in London. She started working as a waitress, but soon modeled for cheesecake photographers. In 1955 comedian Arthur Askey needed a voluptuous blonde for his TV program *Before Your Very Eyes*. It was Askey who renamed her Sabrina (after the Audrey Hepburn movie). Her appearance on the show (although she never uttered a word) was a huge success. Sabrina received a thousand fan letters a week, and movie offers were coming in. It was also the first time British national television was allowed to show cleavage. Dressing in tight and revealing costumes, Sabrina's name soon became synonymous with the word "bosom." She made her debut in *Stock Car* (1955). Again, her voice wasn't heard,

because a Cockney accent was dubbed in over Sabrina's own voice. A cameo in Askey's *Ramsbottom Rides Again* (1956) and a walk-on part in Norman Wisdom's *Just My Luck* (1957) followed. About the former, British *Picturegoer* magazine wrote: "Sabrina, too, wanders through, practically wordless, now and then. But you barely notice her!" Sabrina then took to singing in nightclubs and in April she was seen in a revue called *Pleasures of Paris* (1957). In late 1958 Sabrina left for Australia. She made a personal tour and starred at the Tivoli Theatre in Sydney in her "Pleasure in Paris" show. A year later she left for the United States. Until 1963

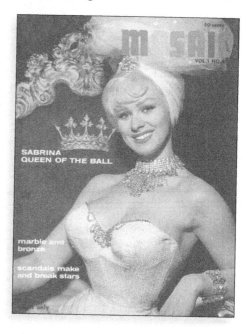

she toured the country singing in nightclubs, making side trips to Cuba, Canada and Venezuela. She made her first American film in 1962. The cult classic *Satan in High Heels* starred her as herself, a nightclub singer in Meg Myles nightclub. In 1967 she married Dr Harold Melsheimer, a wealthy Hollywood plastic surgeon. When Jayne Mansfield died, the part she had signed for in the sleazy horror movie *The Ice House* (1969) was taken by Sabrina. The story is about a

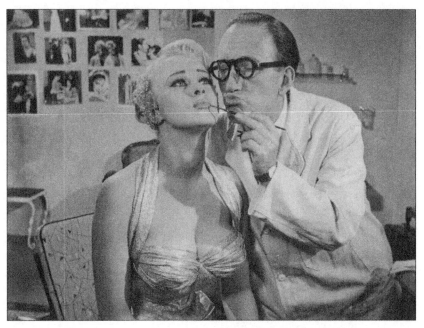

WITH SIDNEY JAMES IN *MAKE MINE A MILLION*, 1959 (BRITISH LION).

serial killer who freezes his victims in ice blocks at the ice house where he works. Sabrina, looking very beautiful, was one of his victims. She separated from Dr Melsheimer in 1977. Sabrina still lives in the United States today.

SABRINA FILMOGRAPHY

1955: *Stock Car* (Trixie).
1956: *Ramsbottom Rides Again* (attractive girl at table).
1957: *Just My Luck* (herself), *Blue Murder at St. Trinians* (Virginia).
1959: *Make Mine a Million* (client).
1962: *Satan in High Heels* (herself, nightclub singer).
1965: *House of the Black Death* (belly dancer).
1969: *The Ice House* (Venus De Marco).
1970: *The Phantom Gunslinger* (Margie).

Sara Shane

Sara Shane was born Elaine Sterling in Kirkwood, Missouri, on May 18, 1928. As a teenager she was a Powers model, which eventually led to some showgirl parts in MGM musicals. In 1949 she married millionaire William I. Hollingsworth and concentrated on married life. In 1955 she returned to acting. As Sara Shane she was under contract to Universal, made two films there and freelanced for a while. She was good in Clark Gable's *The King and Four Queens* (1956) as the youngest of Eleanor Parker's three sisters-in-law. In 1957 she divorced Hollingsworth and went to Cuba to shoot her next project, *Affair in Havana*. She played the young wife of crippled Raymond Burr who has an affair with songwriter John Cassavetes. A couple of television appearances (*The*

WITH JOHN CASSAVETES IN *AFFAIR IN HAVANA*, 1957 (ALLIED ARTISTS).

TARZAN'S GREATEST ADVENTURE, 1959 (PARAMOUNT).

WITH JEFF CHANDLER, JACK PALANCE, CHARLES HORVATH AND RITA GAM IN *SIGN OF THE PAGAN*, 1954 (UNIVERSAL).

Bob Cummings Show, Dragnet, both 1957) and a part in one of the best entries in the *Tarzan* series followed. In 1962 she left for Europe, where she lived in London, Paris and Rome for a while. Back in the US, she moved into the real-estate business. Sara Shane went to Australia in 1980, and still lives there.

WITH KATHLEEN HUGHES IN *THREE BAD SISTERS*, 1956 (UNITED ARTISTS).

SARA SHANE FILMOGRAPHY

1948: *Easter Parade* (showgirl), *Julia Misbehaves* (Mannequin).
1949: *Neptune's Daughter* (Miss Pratt).
1954: *Sign of the Pagan* (Myra), *Magnificent Obsession* (Valerie).
1955: *Daddy Long Legs* (Pat, chorus girl).
1956: *The King and Four Queens* (Oralie McDade), *Three Bad Sisters* (Lorna Craigh).
1957: *Affair in Havana* (Lorna).
1959: *Tarzan's Greatest Adventure* (Angie).

JUNE, 1958

People today

A HILLMAN PUBLICATION

STILL 15¢

DENNIS
CROSBY'S
Best
Girl

For more on
Pat Sheehan
←
see Pages
41-43

Pat Sheehan

Patricia Ann Sheehan was born on September 7, 1931, in San Francisco, California. Her father, Arthur Edmond Sheehan, was an automotive engineer and her mother, Gladys Anna Larson, worked at a hospital. Her parents were divorced in 1935. In 1949 she won the local 'Miss Milkmaid' pageant. At nineteen she was crowned Miss San Francisco. Pat Sheehan was a Las Vegas showgirl, made a couple of movies in the fifties and was a *Playboy* playmate in October 1958 (together with actress Mara Corday). In 1956 she was called NBC's answer to Marilyn Monroe, while appearing in *The Colgate Comedy Hour*. This show really put her name up there, and in a 1956 magazine article she proclaimed, "From now on my parts will be larger. I'm so excited!" What really happened was less exciting; she got no more movie roles (except a cameo in *Gigi*, 1958) and was seen sporadically on television. She did date many famous men, including Frank Sinatra, Howard Hughes and Bing Crosby; but settled down with the latter's son, Dennis Crosby (whom she was married to from 1958 'til 1964). Together, they had two sons. From an earlier marriage, to actor's agent George Von Douglas-Ittu, she had a son which Dennis Crosby adopted in 1958. On January 14, 2006, Pat Sheehan died from a heart attack in Beverly Hills, California.

PAT SHEEHAN FILMOGRAPHY

1954: *The French Line* (model), *The Adventures of Hajji Baba* (handmaiden).
1955: *Daddy Long Legs* (blonde), *Guys and Dolls* (Goldwyn Girl), *Man with the Gun* (saloon girl), *Kismet* (harem girl).
1958: *Gigi* (blonde).

KISMET, 1955 (MGM).

WITH ANGIE DICKINSON, BARBARA LAWRENCE AND JAN STERLING IN *MAN WITH THE GUN*, 1955 (UNITED ARTISTS).

Leigh Snowden

Another star of the Universal stable was blue-eyed, five-foot six-inch-tall Leigh Snowden. They starred her in some dramas and science-fiction films all other Universal starlets were also offered. She was born Martha Lee Estes, on June 23, 1929, in Memphis, Tennessee, of Scottish-Irish descent. When still a young child, her father died and Leigh moved with her mother to Covington, Tennessee. In 1952 she spent the summer with a light opera company which was playing at the Memphis Open Air Theatre. Also in 1952, she married taxi driver Jimmy Snowden and would have two children with him. In 1953 Leigh went off to study voice in San Francisco. While she did so she continued to earn a living as a fashion model. Already a divorced woman, she moved to Los Angeles in 1954. First, she accepted a role in Robert Aldrich's crime classic *Kiss Me Deadly* (1955), as a sexy girl by the swimming pool. It was comedian Jack Benny who gave Leigh

HOT ROD RUMBLE, 1957 (ALLIED ARTISTS).

WITH JEFF MORROW IN *THE CREATURE WALKS AMONG US*, 1956 (UNIVERSAL).

her chance on his television program. She was given a walk-on part in his show. She was an instant hit with the (male) public and was flooded with film offers afterwards. It was Universal who got to sign her up for a long-term contract. She explained that she chose this studio because she knew of its policy of developing talent and grooming young players for stardom. After some parts in programmers like *The Creature Walks Among Us* and *Outside the Law* (both 1956), Leigh

KISS ME DEADLY, 1955 (UNITED ARTISTS).

Snowden requested her release from Universal. She married accordionist Dick Contino on September 18, 1956 and after a leading role in Allied Artists' *Hot Rod Rumble* (1957) she retired from acting. She and Contino had three children. In the sixties she performed as a singer with Contino and made a last (uncredited) appearance in *The Comancheros* (1961). On May 11, 1982, she died of cancer.

LEIGH SNOWDEN FILMOGRAPHY

1955: *Kiss Me Deadly* (girl at swimming pool), *All That Heaven Allows* (Jo-Ann), *Francis in the Navy* (Nurse Appleby).
1956: *Riddles in Rhythm* (herself), *The Creature Walks Among Us* (Marcia Barton), *I've Lived Before* (Lois Gordon), *Outside the Law* (Maria Craven), *The Square Jungle* (Lorraine Evans), *The Rawhide Years* (Miss Vanilla Bissell), *Rebel in Town.*
1957: *Hot Rod Rumble* (Terri Warren).
1961: *The Comancheros* (Evie, hotel girl).

Helene Stanton

Helene Stanton was born Eleanor Stansbury, on November 4, 1925, in Philadelphia, Pennsylvania. From the age of 13, she took singing lessons. She sang for the Cosmopolitan Opera Company in Philadelphia, when, in 1943, she was asked to sing in the stage version of *The Merry Widow*. When she left for Hollywood, she was persuaded to switch from classical to popular music. In 1949 she married former silent-era actor Kenneth Harlan, who was more than twice her senior. Helene was his sixth wife! On December 28, 1953, she obtained a divorce from Harlan. After her divorce she concentrated on singing again and became very good friends with songwriter Jimmy McHugh (who had discovered Mamie Van Doren a year earlier). In 1955 her performance in Las Vegas was seen by an Allied Artists producer, and she was offered a film part in the *film noir* classic *The Big Combo*. After *The Big Combo*, she dyed her brunette hair blonde, and was picked up by Columbia for their *Jungle Jim* series adventure movie, *Jungle Moon Men*, playing the evil jungle high priestess Oma, opposite Johnny Weissmuller. After a small role, as a temperamental movie star declining to play a part in Manning Studios' upcoming epic feature, in Universal's *Four Girls in Town* 1957), she married physician Morton Pinsky and quit acting. The couple had two children together.

HELENE STANTON FILMOGRAPHY

1955: *The Big Combo* (Rita), *New Orleans Uncensored* (Alma Mae), *Jungle Moon Men* (Oma), *Sudden Danger* (Vera), *The Phantom from 10,000 Leagues* (Wanda).
1957: *Four Girls in Town* (Rita Holloway).

JUNGLE MOON MEN, 1955 (COLUMBIA).

SUDDEN DANGER, 1955 (ALLIED ARTISTS).

WITH ARTHUR FRANZ AND MICHAEL GRANGER IN *NEW ORLEANS UNCENSORED,*
1955 (COLUMBIA).

Karen Steele

Once called "One of the most striking actresses to work in show business," Karen Steele, born on March 20, 1931, was a Hawaiian-born blonde who spoke English, Polynesian and Japanese. Karen arrived in Hollywood in the early fifties. She was doing some secretarial work when she met comedian Groucho Marx. It was he who introduced her to the film business. In 1953 she made her movie debut in *The Clown*. This was followed by a small role in the low-budget drama *Man Crazy* (1953). She was out of work for a year, but after her part of Ernest Borgnine's sister-in-law in United Artists' *Marty* (1955), her career really took off. She was offered roles by different studios and in 1957 worked for director Budd Boetticher in his *Decision at Sund*own. Although it is said that she married Boetticher, the truth is that they dated but never married. (In

THE SHARKFIGHTERS, 1956 (UNITED ARTISTS).

WITH COLLEEN MILLER, JOE TURKEL AND CHRISTINE WHITE IN *MAN CRAZY*, 1953 (SECURITY PICTURES).

WITH JOHN PAYNE IN *BAILOUT AT 43,000*, 1957 (UNITED ARTISTS).

WITH RAY DANTON IN *THE RISE AND FALL OF LEGS DIAMOND*, 1960 (WARNER
BROS.).

1960 Boetticher married actress Debra Paget.) They did make more movies together. In *Ride Lonesome* (1959), she was a young widow who is one of the party traveling with Randolph Scott and his prisoner, James Best. The last of her Boetticher parts was in *The Rise and Fall of Legs Diamond* (1960), with Ray Danton. She was the dancing teacher who enters a dancing competition with Diamond after (unknown to her) he had disabled her dancing partner. Karen was considered to star opposite Elvis Presley in Flaming Star (1960). She eventually lost the part to blonde newcomer Barbara Eden. (Later, she lost another role to Eden; the starring part in television's *I Dream of Jeannie*.) A year of many television appearances followed, before she returned to the big screen for a Tony Curtis comedy called *40 Pounds of Trouble* (1962), playing a girl called Bambi! The rest of her acting career was mostly on television. On March 12, 1988, she died in Kingman, Arizona, leaving her husband Dr. Maurice Boyd Ruland behind.

KAREN STEELE FILMOGRAPHY

1953: *The Clown* (blonde), *Man Crazy* (Marge).

1955: *Marty* (Virginia).

1956: *Toward the Unknown* (Polly Craven), *The Sharkfighters* (Martha Staves).

1957: *Bailout at 43,000* (Carol Petersen), *Decision at Sundown* (Lucy Summerton).

1959: *Westbound* (Jeanie Miller), *Ride Lonesome* (Mrs. Lane).

1960: *The Rise and Fall of Legs Diamond* (Alice Shiffer).

1962: *40 Pounds of Trouble* (Bambi).

1966: *Cyborg 2087* (Dr. Sharon Mason).

1969: *A Boy...a Girl* (Elizabeth).

1972: *The Trap on Cougar Mountain.*

Venetia Stevenson

British-born Joanna Venetia Stevenson (London, March 10, 1938) is the daughter of director Robert Stevenson and actress Anna Lee. When she is only 18 months old, her father, directing a movie in the United States, takes his wife and daughter with him. Following her parents' divorce in March of 1944, Venetia chose to live with her father. Before making a name for herself in show business, she married actor Russ Tamblyn, at age seventeen, in 1956. Only one year later the couple separated. After several television appearances and a small role in RKO's *The Girl Most Likely* (1957), she was signed by Warner Bros. In *Island of Lost Women* (1959), she is one of three sisters (June Blair and Diane Jergens were the others) who live

with their father on a desolate island. When a plane crash brings two handsome men to their island, Venetia finds romance with rugged Jeff Richards. Because she didn't like the roles offered to her, she asked to be released from her contact in 1959. Being estranged from her mother for fifteen years, she was reunited with her after appearing with her in the films *Jet Over the Atlantic* (1959) and *The Big Night* (1960). Some Westerns and B-movies later, she left her showbiz career to marry Everly Brother Don in 1962. She told *Picturegoer* magazine in 1958: "I'm no dedicated actress. I'll marry again when the real thing comes along." Apparently, Don Everly wasn't the real thing, because the couple divorced in 1970. Venetia became a script reader for actor and friend Burt Reynolds's movie production company in the late seventies and became the vice-president of the film production company "Cinema Group." Venetia Stevenson never remarried.

DARBY'S RANGERS, 1958 (WARNER BROS.).

WITH MARTIN WEST IN *THE SERGEANT WAS A LADY*, 1961 (UNIVERSAL).

VENETIA STEVENSON FILMOGRAPHY

1957: *The Girl Most Likely*.

1958: *Violent Road* (Doreen), *Darby's Rangers* (Peggy McTavish).

1959: *Island of Lost Women* (Venus), *Day of the Outlaw* (Ernine).

1960: *Jet Over the Atlantic* (June Elliott), *The Big Night* (Ellie), *City of the Dead/Horror Hotel* (Nan Barlow), *Seven Ways from Sundown* (Joy Karrington), *Studs Lonigan* (Lucy Scanlon).

1961: *The Sergeant Was a Lady* (Sgt. Judy Fraser).

WITH JOHN SMITH, JUNE BLAIR AND JEFF RICHARDS IN *ISLAND OF LOST WOMEN*, 1959 (WARNER BROS.).

Sally Todd

Sally Todd was the *Playboy* Playmate of the Month in February 1957. She had earlier appeared in that magazine, but that story didn't contain nudity. She was born Sally Jo Todd, on June 7, 1934, in Tucson, Arizona. With encouragement from her mother, she entered the 1955 "Miss Tucson Beauty Contest" and won first prize, which was a trip to Hollywood. Shortly after arriving in the film capitol, she landed herself a job as a "Carson Cutie" on television's *The Johnny Carson Show* (1955). Then 20th Century-Fox took her in for a cameo part in Sheree North's *The Best Things in Life are Free* (1956) and cast her as a dance hall hostess in *The Revolt of Mamie Stover* (1956), with Jane Russell and fellow blonde Kathy Marlowe. The 20th Century-Fox publicity department publicized her as "A young Lana Turner and much prettier than Marilyn Monroe." Before the *Playboy* layout, she posed for many cheesecake layouts in magazines like *Bachelor* and *Brief*. A

FRANKENSTEIN'S DAUGHTER, 1958 (ASTOR PICTURES).

couple of featured roles in low-budget horror movies (*The Unearthly* and *Franken-stein's Daughter*, both 1957) didn't do much for her career either. She later said that she took these roles until something better would come along. Sally was romanti-cally linked to several Hollywood actors. She dated Jack Webb in 1958 (before he married actress Jackie Loughery), and there were even rumors of a Mexican mar-riage to Vince Edwards. On August 26 1958, Sally Todd was arrested for drunk

WITH TOR JOHNSON IN *THE UNEARTHLY*, 1957 (REPUBLIC).

driving and causing a freeway accident involving five other cars. She was held in prison for one day. After a cameo in Elvis Presley's *G.I. Blues* (1960) and a couple of television appearances (e.g. *The Untouchables* and *77 Sunset Strip*), she quit acting in 1961 for married life. Her first marriage was to singer Charles Cochran (Octo-ber 1961), but that only lasted a few months. On June 8, 1963, she married CBS engineer John W. James in Las Vegas. The couple is still married to this day.

SALLY TODD FILMOGRAPHY

1956: *The Best Things in Life are Free* (chorus girl), *The Revolt of Mamie Stover* (dance hall hostess).
1957: *The Unearthly* (Natalie Anders), *Viking Women and the Sea Serpent* (Sanda).
1958: *Fraulein* (blonde pin-up on poster in bedroom), *Frankenstein's Daughter* (Suzy Lawler).
1959: *Al Capone* (beautiful blonde).
1960: *G.I. Blues* (bargirl).

Mamie Van Doren

Mamie Van Doren is one of the last surviving fifties blondes. Still platinum blonde, Mamie hosts her own website and sells topless photos of herself at age 77! She was born Joan Lucille Olander in Rowena, South Dakota, on February 6, 1933. The Olanders originated from Europe. They once lived in Holland (Olander had once been "Hollander," which means Dutchman), moved to Sweden and finally settled in the United States. At age nine Mamie moved to Los Angeles with her family. After being crowned "Miss Palm Springs," RKO's Howard Hughes signed her to a contract. Mamie made her debut in *Jet Pilot*. The movie was filmed in 1949, but not released until 1957. In 1950 she met Jack Newman, married him and divorced him after their honeymoon, because he tried to throw her off a balcony! After a couple of bit parts in RKO musicals, she had a small role in the stage show *Million Dollar Baby* (1951). She turned to singing in night-

clubs, where agent Jimmy McHugh saw her and arranged for her to do a screen test at Paramount in 1952. Although the test was received enthusiastically, Paramount executives decided not to place Mamie under contract because of her resemblance to Marilyn Monroe. They thought it would be too hard to market her in competition with 20th Century-Fox's blonde bombshell. At least that was their official statement. In her autobiography, *Playing the Field*, Mamie claims that Jimmy McHugh's lover, Hollywood gossip columnist Louella Parsons, was jealous of her and rang Paramount to ban all Paramount's stars and productions from her well-read nationwide columns, if they hired

the talents of starlet Joan Olander. Instead, she took a role in the play *Come Back, Little Sheba*. One night there was a Universal studios talent scout in the audience. He contacted Jimmy McHugh, and when it was confirmed that Mamie could sing as well, she got a small part as a nightclub singer in their upcoming Tony Curtis vehicle *Forbidden*. Jimmy managed to get Mamie signed to a seven-year contract with two-year options. (Miss Parsons was in Europe during this time!)

WITH KATHLEEN CASE, WILLIAM CAMPBELL AND JAN MERLIN IN *RUNNING WILD*, 1955 (UNIVERSAL).

She had a nice role in *The All American* (1954) and was a harem girl in *Yankee Pasha* that same year. Mamie received some good press reviews for these two parts. *Variety* wrote about *The All American*: "A different kind of appeal — than that of Lori Nelson — was meant in the casting of Mamie Van Doren, blonde charmer who lures the players to an off-limits beer joint and gets them in trouble. She's up to the role's demands." And about her role in *Yankee Pasha*, *Variety* wrote, "Mamie Van Doren, Universal's Monroe-ish blonde curve-pitcher, stirs up some chuckles as a talkative harem slave." She was given the tag of "poor man's Lana Turner" around this time, because the press thought there was a resemblance between the two stars. *Running Wild* (1955) marked her first juvenile film appearance. Universal was one of the first studios to discover that teenagers and their music were exploitable in films. Mamie commented later, "I didn't want to make this film. First, it was in black and white, a comedown after doing several movies in color. And it was a role that I thought was out of character for me — a 'bad'

WITH ERIC MASON IN *THE CANDIDATE*, 1964 (COSNAT PRODUCTIONS).

girl.'" Looking back, the funny thing is that the "bad girl" tag was the one that made Mamie famous and unforgettable to picturegoers then *and* now! On August 29, 1955, Mamie married bandleader Ray Anthony. In 1953 he had written a song about Marilyn Monroe, and he did the same for his wife when he wrote "M-m-m-Mamie." Six months after the marriage, their son Perry was born. While pregnant Mamie starred in a quality Western *Star in the Dust* (1956), with John

WITH JOHN RUSSELL IN *UNTAMED YOUTH*, 1957 (WARNER BROS.).

Agar. Because of her marriage and becoming a mother, Mamie was dropped by Universal. Her contract ended in 1957, and she was able to continue her acting and ballet lessons at Universal, but was not hired for any more film parts there. Nevertheless, Mamie found herself a lot of work during the next three years. She appeared in movies like *The Girl in Black Stockings* (1957) for United Artists. Well advertised, she had a small part as the victim of a craze murderer. UK's *Picture-goer* magazine wrote in its review: "Mamie Van Doren — as luscious as a pink ice-cream — is added as a sweetener." This B suspense thriller was followed by *Untamed Youth* (1957) for Warner Bros., a classic in the teenage genre, with Mamie singing some great songs written by Eddie Cochran; *Teacher's Pet* (1958) for Paramount, together with Clark Gable and Doris Day; and *High School Confidential!* (1958) for MGM, in which she played "the aunt" of Russ Tamblyn who wore her sweaters a couple of sizes too small and comes on to her nephew every scene they have together. Her marriage was falling apart, and when Mamie left

WITH RUSS TAMBLYN IN *HIGH SCHOOL CONFIDENTIAL*, 1958 (MGM).

WITH CLARK GABLE IN *TEACHER'S PET*, 1958 (PARAMOUNT).

WITH MICKEY ROONEY IN *THE PRIVATE LIVES OF ADAM AND EVE,* 1960
(UNIVERSAL).

THREE NUTS IN SEARCH OF A BOLT, 1964 (HARLEQUIN INTERNATIONAL
PICTURES).

for Italy to film *La Bellissime Gambe di Sabrina* in 1958, Ray Anthony didn't accompany her. The couple decided to break up, and in 1961 their divorce became final. A free woman now, Mamie had the time of her life in Italy. She romanced her co-star Antonio Cifariello, who was a popular star in Italy in those days. Back in the United States, she played a victim of rapist Ray Danton in *The Beat Generation* (1959), and *Girls Town* had her locked up in a girl's reformatory. Mamie was

WITH RAY ANTHONY IN *GIRLS' TOWN*, 1959 (MGM).

back at Universal for *The Private Lives of Adam and Eve* (1960) and went to Argentina to film *Una Americana en Buenos Aires* with Jean-Pierre Aumont in 1961. In 1962 she made an appearance on TV in *The Dick Powell Show* and had a part in the stage musical *Wildcat*, followed by another play, *Silk Stockings* (1963). It was during *Wildcat* that Mamie learned that Marilyn Monroe had died. In her autobiography she wrote that with Monroe's death, the era of the blonde sex goddesses had also passed away. She then was offered, but declined, a part opposite Jayne Mansfield in *Promises, Promises!* (1963). Mamie's first film in over three years, was *Party Girls for the Candidate* (1964). It was later renamed *The Candidate*, and bosomy blonde June Wilkinson also starred. The two actresses became friends, and recorded a single, "Bikini with No Top on the Top." She gained more publicity when Tommy Noonan asked her to appear nude in his *Three Nuts in Search of a Bolt* (1964); Mamie was featured in *Playboy* magazine with photos that were shot while filming her nude beer bath scene. She then left for Germany to appear

WITH DONALD O'CONNOR IN *FRANCIS JOINS THE WACS*, 1954 (UNIVERSAL).

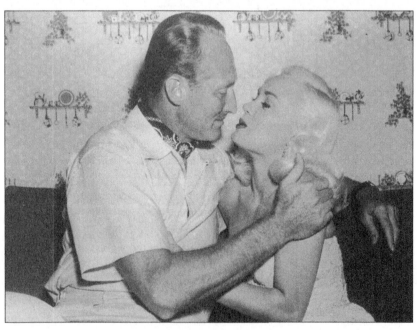

WITH JOHN HOLLAND IN *THE GIRL IN BLACK STOCKINGS*, 1957 (UNITED ARTISTS).

in *Freddy und das Lied der Prärie* with German singer/actor Freddy Quinn. Between 1964 and 1965, Mamie published three paperback books about her (love) life. In their time these pocket books were quite sensational for their stories about the sexual escapades of famous Hollywood actors and Mamie's daring quotes. For example: "I am sure that the average girl would have a sexual appetite like mine if she were thrown into the kind of world I've been in, so I have no guilt." She was booked for some nightclub performances in the United States, had appeared in *Playboy* twice (February and June 1964) and made a couple of mediocre movies with titles like *The Navy vs. the Night Monsters* (1966) and *You've Got to be Smart* (1967). She had the better part in *Las Vegas Hillbillys* (1966), while Jayne Mansfield made a guest appearance. The movie itself was a cheaply made comedy full of country music stars. It was the first time that the two blondes were seen together in a movie or play. Sometimes they filled in each other's assignments, when one was unavailable to appear. Mamie was married to 19-year-old California Angels' pitcher Lee Meyers from 1966 'til 1967 (She was 33 years old at that time!) In 1968 she toured Vietnam to entertain the servicemen there, and went back to Vietnam again in 1971. After Vietnam, Mamie decided to take a chance of refreshing her career in England. She moved to London, but there was no work for her in the English theatres or the movie business, and she returned to the United States just six months later. In 1972 Mamie toured the country in a play that was originally a star vehicle for former blonde rival Jayne Mansfield, *Will Success Spoil Rock Hunter?* (In her autobiography Mamie says she was the first choice for the Broadway play back in 1956. She supposedly turned it down because the role of blonde actress Rita Marlow put the attention too much on her comparison with Marilyn Monroe. She thought it would harm her career.) Another short-lived marriage was with corporate executive Ross McLintock (1972-1973). Her fifties sexpot image had reached its decline by now. Mamie was cast in "naughty"-themed plays (e.g. In *One Bed and Out the Other*, 1974) and a low-budget movie for director/producer Matt Cimber. Cimber was the third husband of Jayne Mansfield. Jayne had originally been offered the part (in the late sixties) that Mamie eventually played in *That Girl from Boston* (1975). The film was based on the pulp novel by Robert H. Rimmer, published in 1962. Well in her forties now, Mamie struggled in showbiz land to get some decent work. On June 26, 1979, she married her fifth (and last) husband, actor Thomas Dixon, who's thirteen years her junior and who co-starred with her in the Florida tour of *Will Success Spoil Rock Hunter?* in 1974. In the mid-eighties Mamie was rediscovered by a new generation of fans. She made a couple of movies, was seen on TV talk shows, posed for *Playboy* again (at age 53) and released her autobiography, *Playing the Field*, in 1987. Twenty years later, Mamie is still making news and keeps in contact with her fans from all over the world, through the medium of the Internet.

BELGIAN POSTER FOR *THE ALL AMERICAN,* **1953 (UNIVERSAL).**

1951: *Footlight Varieties* (blonde in theatre), *His Kind of Woman* (girl in bar of lodge), *Two Tickets to Broadway* (showgirl), *Jet Pilot* (dancing girl).

1953: *Forbidden* (nightclub singer), *The All American* (Susie Ward).

1954: *Hawaiian Nights, Francis Joins the WACS* (Lt. Bunky Hilstrom), *Yankee Pasha* (slavegirl Lilith).

1955: *Ain't Misbehavin'* (Jackie), *The Second Greatest Sex* (Birdie Snyder), *Running Wild* (Irma Bean).

1956: *Star in the Dust* (Ellen Ballard).

1957: *The Girl in Black Stockings* (Harriet Ames), *Untamed Youth* (Penny Lowe).

1958: *Teacher's Pet* (Peggy DeFore), *High School Confidential!* (Gwen Dulaine), *Le Bellissime Gambe di Sabrina/The Beautiful Legs of Sabrina* (Sabrina).

1959: *The Big Operator* (Mary Gibson), *The Beat Generation* (Georgia Altera), *Girls Town* (Silver Morgan), *Born Reckless* (Jackie Adams), *Guns, Girls and Gangsters* (Vi Victor), *Vice Raid* (Carol Hudson).

1960: *College Confidential* (Sally Blake), *The Private Lives of Adam and Eve* (Evie Simms), *Sex Kittens Go to College* (Dr. Mathilda West).

1961: *Una Americana en Buenos Aires/The Blonde From Buenos Aires.*

1964: *The Candidate* (Samantha Ashley), *Three Nuts in Search of a Bolt* (Saxie Symbol, the Tallahassee tassel tosser), *Freddy und das Lied der Prärie/The Sheriff was a Lady* (Olivia).

1966: *Las Vegas Hillbillys* (Boots Malone), *The Navy vs. the Night Monsters* (Nora Hall).

1967: *You've Got to be Smart* (Lynn Hathaway).

1968: *Voyage to the Planet of Prehistoric Women* (Moana).

1971: *I Fratelli di Arizona/The Arizona Kid* (Sharon Miller).

1975: *That Girl from Boston.*

1986: *Free Ride* (Debbie Stockwell).

1987: *Glory Years* (Minnie).

1993: *King B: a Life in the Movies.*

1999: *The Vegas Connection* (Rita).

2002: *Slackers* (Mrs. Van Graaf).

Joan Vohs

Blue-eyed Elinor Joan Vohs was born on July 30, 1927, in St. Albans, New York. She became the Rockettes' youngest chorine at age 16 and was a Conover model (she was 5 feet 6 inches tall) afterwards. On Broadway she was seen as one of the dancers in the musical *Follow the Girls* (1945-1946) with Jackie Gleason, and had a larger role in the comedy *Parlor Story* (1947). Unluckily for Joan, the play only lasted 23 performances. Hoping to have more luck in the movies, she moved to Los Angeles. She landed herself a contract at Warner Bros. studios in 1949 and played small roles in films for other studios as well 'til 1951. She returned to modeling for a while when movie offers stopped coming. But 1953 had her back on the studio lots; she made three movies that year. In United Artists' *Vice Squad* she played the small role of a prostitute who witnesses

LURE OF THE SWAMP, 1957 (20TH CENTURY FOX).

FRONT ROW: LORRAINE CRAWFORD, LOLA ALBRIGHT, MYRNA DELL, JOI LANSING, JOAN VOHS AND KAREN X. GAYLORD IN *THE GIRL FROM JONES BEACH*, 1949 (WARNER BROS.).

WITH PHYLLIS FOWLER AND GEORGE MONTGOMERY IN *FORT TI*, 1953 (COLUMBIA).

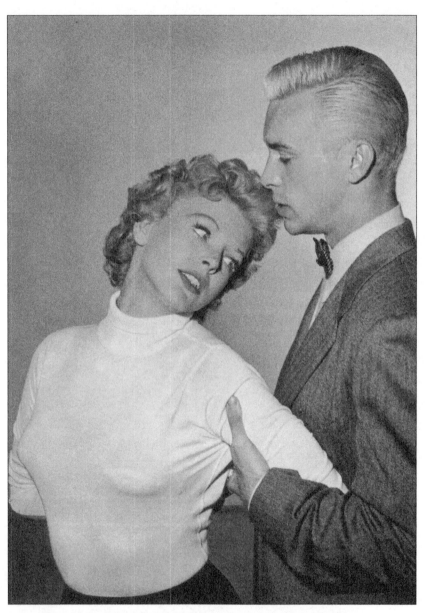

WITH SKIP HOMEIER IN *CRY VENGEANCE*, 1954 (ALLIED ARTISTS).

the killing of a policeman. Edward G. Robinson questions her and her client about the murder. A bigger, but not better, role came with Columbia's *Fort Ti*. In this 3-D adventure movie, set in the 1700s, Joan appeared as a girl suspected of being a French spy. Ranger George Montgomery, who is working with the British, comes to her rescue. In 1954 she played together with Martha Hyer in Allied Artists' *Cry Vengeance*. Miss Hyer was the good girl, and Joan played bad blonde/gun moll Lily. Joan Vohs turned down a part in the Jerry Lewis and Dean Martin comedy *Artists and Models* (1955) because she refused to take another role typecasting her as a dumb blonde. (The role was given to Anita Ekberg.) Joan later commented on her struggle to get rid of the dumb blonde tag: "Once a dumb blonde, always a dumb blonde in the opinion of some of the producers and casting directors." Most of her films were B-movies and in 1957 she made her last motion picture. A lot of television work followed the coming years. In 1959 she married John Stephens. She passed away on June 4, 2001, of heart failure.

JOAN VOHS FILMOGRAPHY

1949: *My Dream is Yours* (party guest), *The Girl from Jones Beach* (Randolph girl), *It's a Great Feeling* (model), *Yes Sir That's My Baby* (Mrs. Flugeldorfer).
1950: *Girls' School* (Jane Ellen), *County Fair* (Phyllis).
1951: *Royal Wedding* (dancer), *I'll See You in my Dreams* (chorus girl), *As You Were* (sergeant).
1953: *Crazylegs* (Ruth), *Fort Ti* (Fortune Mallory), *Vice Squad* (Vickie Webb).
1954: *Cry Vengeance* (Lily Arnold), *Sabrina* (Gretchen van Horn).
1955: *Fort Yuma* (Melanie Crown).
1956: *Terror at Midnight* (Susan Lang).
1957: *Lure of the Swamp* (Cora Payne).

Sheree Winton

British blonde Sheree Winton made a name for herself posing bikini clad in several men's magazines before starting out in films. She was born Shirley Patrick on November 4, 1935, in Sheffield. At sixteen she left home, ultimately settling in London a year later. There she worked as a receptionist in a detective agency. She married Mr. Winner (who was 21 years her senior) and made him change his name to Winton. In 1954 she gave birth to her son, Dale, who has become a famous television actor/presenter in Britain. She made her debut on Michael Miles's TV show *Take Your Pick*, dressed in a mink bikini. Sheree was seen on TV with then-famous British comedians (Bruce Forsyth, Roy Hudd and Bob Monkhouse) and had small roles in some movies, mostly cast as a chorus girl or just a beauti-

ful blonde. After she appeared on the *Benny Hill Show* on television, she was cast as Laurence Olivier's man-chasing mistress in *The Devil's Discipline* (1959). At 24 she underwent breast surgery. She became so well-endowed, it caused a strain on her back. In the 1960s she was seen mostly on television with comedians Terry-Thomas and Frankie Howerd, or playing on the London stage. In 1965 she was seen together with Margaret Rutherford and Sidney James in *The Solid Gold Cadillac*. In 1967 she divorced Gary Winton. Suffering from depression and insomnia in her late thirties, she took her own life on May 28, 1976.

To Peter
Best wishes
Sheree
Winton

WITH JOSEPHINE LISLE, RONALD SHINER, SHANE CORDELL AND MARIE
DEVEREUX IN *GIRLS AT SEA*, 1958 (ABPC).

SHEREE WINTON FILMOGRAPHY

1957: *Miracle in Soho* (blonde).

1958: *Girls at Sea* (bathing girl), *The Two-Headed Spy* (blonde at party).

1959: *Follow a Star* (showgirl), *The Rough and the Smooth/Portrait of a Sinner*
(prostitute), *Naked Fury* (bargirl), *First Man into Space* (nurse in blood
bank), *The Devil's Disciple* (blonde mistress).

1960: *Dentist in the Chair* (Jayne).

1961: *The Pursuers.*

1962: *The Road to Hong Kong.*

1964: *A Hard Day's Night.*

1965: *Thunderball.*

1969: *Rhubarb* (Lady Pupil Rhubarb), *The Assassination Bureau* (La Belle Amie
girl).

Yana

Yana was already a well-known song-stress before she turned to acting. Mostly cast as a singer in her movies, Yana had a fan following during her days of acting fame. She was born Pamela Guard on February 16, 1932, in Romford, Great Britain. This one-time hair stylist and model started out singing in London cafes. Her tiny debut part, in *The Ship that Died of Shame* (1955), was followed by a small part in *The Cockleshell Heroes* (1956), which was only seen in the States (she was cut out of the British version). Warwick studios even sent her on a fourteen-week tour to sell the movie to the US audience. She was seen by 50 million people on television on the Bob Hope and Ed Sullivan shows. But that, and all the press coverage and personal appearances, didn't lead to any movie work in the States. Back in England, she returned to singing and played the leading part in the stage musical *Cinderella* (1958) at the London Coliseum with Tommy Steele. Yana died in London on November 21, 1989.

YANA FILMOGRAPHY

1955: *The Ship that Died of Shame.*
1956: *The Cockleshell Heroes, Zarak.*
1957: *Interpol/Pickup Alley* (singer).

Other Fifties Blondes

The following ladies were also blonde and sultry in (some of) their movie roles. I've included them in these mini-bio and filmographies because they are well remembered and appreciated by fans of fifties movie blondes.

LOLA ALBRIGHT

Lola Albright was born on July 20, 1925, in Akron, Ohio. After modeling and working for a radio station in Akron, she moved to Hollywood in the mid-1940s. She got a starlet contract at MGM and appeared with Dolores Donlon, Sara Shane and Joy Lansing in *Easter Parade* (1948) as models. Later, she was featured with Kirk Douglas in the 1949 hit *Champion*. From 1958 to 1961 she played nightclub singer Edie Hart in the popular TV series *Peter Gunn*. Lola Albright briefly played Constance McKenzie in the soap opera *Peyton Place* (1964) after Dorothy Malone became ill and could no longer play the role. Other films: *The Girl from Jones Beach* (1949), *Beauty on Parade* (1950), *The Silver Whip* (1953), *The Tender Trap* (1956), *Pawnee* (1957), *Seven Guns to Mesa* (1958), *A Cold Wind in August* (1961) and *Lord Love a Duck* (1966).

CARROLL BAKER

Carroll Baker (born on May 28, 1931 in Johnstown, Pennsylvania) started her movie career in the fifties, but played her sexiest roles in the sixties. After her movie debut, she left Hollywood to play in two Broadway plays, *Escapade* (1953) and *All Summer Long* (1954). Warner Brothers put her under contract because they sensed a new Monroe in her. Her role in *Baby Doll* (1956) gave her fame and ranked her between the sexy stars of those days, but her other fifties parts were disappointing. Not that Miss Baker didn't act well in them, but because her roles were serious ones and didn't do much at the box office. Some of her movies: *Easy to Love* (1953), *But Not for Me* (1959), *Something Wild* (1961), *Station Six-Sahara* (1962), *The Carpetbaggers* (1964), *Sylvia, Harlow* (both 1965).

MAY BRITT

Swedish Maybritt Wilkens was born on March 22, 1933, in Lindingö. While visiting Sweden, film producer Carlo Ponti and director Maria Soldati were searching for a blonde girl to star in one of their movies. They encountered May in the photographer's shop where she worked. She was only 18 when she made her debut in Soldati's *Jolanda la Figlia del Corsaro Nero* (1952). Many other Italian and French films followed before she came to Hollywood to star in *The Young Lions* (1958) at 20th Century-Fox. Her first US production was Paramount's *War and Peace* (1956), but her scenes were filmed in Europe. She was often typecast as a *femme-fatale*. When Marilyn Monroe declined to do *The Blue Angel* (1959), May Britt played the role that thirties blonde Marlene Dietrich had made famous. After her marriage to Sammy Davis Jr. (1960-1968) she quit acting. Some other films: *La Lupa* (1953), *Ça Va Barder* (1955), *The Hunters* (1958), *Murder Inc.* (1960).

PEGGIE CASTLE

B-movie actress Peggie Castle (real name: Peggy Thomas Blair) was born on December 22, 1927, in Appalachia, Virginia. She was married to Revis Call from 1945 until 1950, and made her movie debut as Peggy Call in Columbia's *When a Girl's Beautiful* (1947). Universal studios signed her to a contract, but her best roles were those made freelancing for different studios: United Artists' *I, the Jury* (1954) and AIP's *The Oklahoma Woman* (1956). In the sixties she developed a drinking problem and died of cirrhosis of the liver on August 11, 1973. Other films: *The Golden Horde* (1951), *Harem Girl* (1952), *The Long Wait* (1954), *Finger Man* (1955), *Miracle in the Rain* (1956) and *Hell's Crossroads* (1957).

DIANE CILENTO

British actress Diane Cilento was born in Brisbane, Queensland, Australia, on October 5, 1933. She was adept at playing tarts with hearts, but found herself in too many unworthy film parts during the fifties. She came from London to Broadway to star as Helen of Troy in *Tiger at the Gates* (October 4, 1955-April 7 1956). For her part in this stage drama she won the Theatre World Award in 1956. Her part in *Tom Jones* (1963) got her nominated for the 1964 Academy Awards as Best Supporting Actress. She's the mother of actor Jason Connery (1963), who was born during her marriage to Sean Connery (1962-1973). Other films: *Wings of Danger* (1952), *Meet Mr. Lucifer* (1953), *Passing Stranger* (1954), *Passage Home* (1955), *The Truth About Women* (1958), *Jet Storm* (1959), *The Naked Edge* (1961) and *I Thank a Fool* (1962).

WITH MERRY ANDERS IN *THE DALTON GIRLS*, 1957.

LISA DAVIS

Actress/singer Lisa Davis (nee Cheryl Davis) was born in Great Britain on April 20, 1936. In 1953 MGM brought her over to Hollywood to play a part in *Young Bess*. She never played in that film, but did take acting lessons at MGM. Columbia later signed her, and there she made her debut in *The Long Gray Line* (1955). After some small roles, she played the roles that made her name: Rose Dalton in *The Dalton Girls* (1957) and Venusian Motya in the cult classic *Queen of Outer Space* (1958). She married her co-star from the latter, Patrick Waltz, in 1958. Other films: *Spy Chasers* (1955), *The Best Things in Life are Free* (both 1956), *Baby Face Nelson* (1957), *Frontier Rangers* and *Don't Give Up the Ship* (both 1959).

MYRNA DELL

Marilyn Adele Dunlap was born on March 5, 1924, in Los Angeles. Although she spent her early years near Hollywood, she became a showgirl in the Earl Carroll Revue in New York at the age of sixteen. She made her film debut in *A Night at Earl Carroll's* (1940). She went back to the Revue for a while and returned to Hollywood in 1943. RKO signed her up and she made one film after another. In the fifties she was seen more and more on television. Some of Miss Dell's movies are: *The Falcon in San Francisco* (1945), *The Locket* (1946), *The Uninvited Blonde* (1948), *The Girl from Jones Beach* (1949), *Secrets of Beauty* (1951), *The Toughest Man Alive* (1955) and *The Naked Hills* (1956).

MYLÈNE DEMONGEOT

Mylène Demongeot started in the film business when the Brigitte Bardot style was all the rage in Europe. She was born Marie-Hélène Demongeot on September 28, 1936 in France. She made her debut at the age of 18 in *Les Enfants de l'Amour* (1954). Her international career took off when she played Yves Montand's mistress in *Les Sorcières de Salem* (*The Witches of Salem*, 1957). She was seen in the States in *Bonjour Tristesse* (1958) and in the United Kingdom she played in a couple of comedies. Some of her films: *Futures Vedettes* (1955), *Sois Belle et tais-toi/Blonde for Danger* (1957), *Upstairs and Downstairs* (1959), *Under Ten Flags*, *The Singer Not the Song* (both 1960), *Doctor in Distress* (1963), *Fantomâs* (1964) and *The Private Navy of Sergeant O'Farrell* (1968).

DOLORES DONLON

Born in September 19, 1926, in Philadelphia, blonde Patricia Vaniver came to Hollywood after being crowned as "Miss Philadelphia" in 1944. She moved to New York and became a model. She was cast in cameo parts in some MGM vehicles and was also busy modeling on the west coast. She was mostly seen on television and only made a few motion pictures. In August 1957 she posed for *Playboy* magazine, and was their Playmate of the Month. Films: *The Doughgirls* (1944), *Big City, Easter Parade* (both 1948), *The Long Wait, Security Risk* (both 1954) and *Flight to Hong Kong* (1956).

JANE EASTON

This blonde starlet was born on February 28, 1927 in Omaha, Nebraska. She appeared in a few movies and had photo spreads in some glamour pictorials in the fifties. Easton was briefly under contract at RKO and Universal. Some of the movies she appeared in: *Jet Pilot* (1949), *The Sound of Fury* (1950), *Two Tickets to Broadway* (1951), *Son of Paleface, The Las Vegas Story* (both 1952), *Abbott and Costello Go to Mars, Serpent of the Nile, Here Come the Girls, City of Bad Men* (all 1953), *The French Line, Bitter Creek* (both 1954), *The Purple Mask, Son of Sinbad* (both 1955). Jane Easton died on January 28, 2008 in New York.

SHIRLEY EATON

"The Golden Girl" from the James Bond movie *Goldfinger* (1964) started making movies at the age of 17. Shirley Eaton was born on January 12, 1937, in London. She studied acting at Aida Fosters' school for dramatic art and was hired to double for Janet Leigh in *Prince Valiant* (1954), an American production filmed in England. She was offered a Rank contract and appeared in some nice comedies during the fifties and early sixties. Playing Jill Masterson in *Goldfinger* (1964) meant her international breakthrough. In Hollywood she appeared in such movies as *Rhino!* (1964) and *Around the World Under the Sea* (1966). Some of her other films: *You Know What Sailors Are, Doctor in the House* (both 1954), *Three Men in a Boat* (1956), *The Naked Truth* (1957), *Carry on Sergeant* (1958), *A Weekend with Lulu, Dentist on the Job* (both 1961) and *The Girl Hunters* (1963).

SALLY FORREST

Fresh out of high school, Catherine Sally Feeney (born on May 28, 1925 in San Diego) was signed by MGM. As Katherine Feeney she danced in a couple of musicals and played small roles in other productions the studio. When actress Ida Lupino spotted her, she offered her a starring role in *Not Wanted* (1949) and changed her name to Sally Forrest. After her marriage (1951) she lost interest in her Hollywood career and faded from the film scene. When Vanessa Brown left the Broadway play *The Seven Year Itch*, Sally stepped in to play "the girl upstairs." Her films include: *Fiesta* (1947), *The Pirate, Easter Parade* (both 1948), *Never Fear* (1949), *Mystery Street* (1950), *Excuse My Dust, Bannerline* (both 1951), *Code Two* (1953), *Son of Sinbad* (1955) and *While the City Sleeps* (1956).

THE AMOROUS PRAWN, 1962.

LIZ FRASER

Bubbly British blonde Liz Fraser (real name: Elizabeth Winch) was born on August 14, 1933, in London. Her first venture into showbiz was in comedian Tony Hancock's TV series, but she really made her name playing dumb blondes in the mid-fifties. She specialized in light comedy and for a while she took the romantic lead in some *Carry On* features. Later on she appeared on the stage in some acclaimed dramatic roles. Among her many movie appearances are: *Touch and Go* (1955), *The Smallest Show on Earth* (1957), *Wonderful Things!* (1958), *Alive and Kicking, I'm All Right Jack* (both 1959), *Doctor in Love* (1960), *Carry On Regardless, Watch it, Sailor!* (both 1961), *The Amorous Prawn* (1962), *Carry on Cabby* (1963) and *The Americanization of Emily* (1964).

ANGELA GREENE

Forties starlet Angela Greene was born Angela Catherine Williams in Dublin, Ireland, on February 24, 1922. Because of the poverty in Ireland, her family decided to leave for the United States in 1928. During the forties, Angela is a well-known pin-up/cover girl. She landed herself some bit parts in a couple of movies, and in the fifties she was a leading actress in B-movies and appeared on television. Some of her films: *Hollywood Canteen* (1944), *Mildred Pierce* (1945), *Cinderella Jones* (1946), *Escape Me Never* (1947), *Wallflower* (1948), *At War with the Army* (1950), *Jungle Jim in the Forbidden Land* (1952), *The Lady Wants Mink* (1953), *Shotgun* (1955), *Affair in Reno* (1957), *Night of the Blood Beast* (1958) and *The Cosmic Man* (1959). Miss Greene died in Los Angeles on February 9, 1978.

MARJORIE HELLEN

Marjorie Hellen is better known under the name Leslie Parrish. Born Marjorie Helen, on March 13, 1935, she was put under contract to 20th Century-Fox in 1955 (*How to be Very, Very Popular, The Virgin Queen, The Lieutenant Wore Skirts*) and was used by MGM for three pictures (*Hot Summer Night, The Opposite Sex*, both 1956, and *Man on Fire*, 1957) the following year. She did a couple of B-movies (*Tank Battalion*, 1958, and *Missile to the Moon*, 1959) before she was cast as Daisy Mae in *Li'l Abner* (1959) at Paramount. Some movies, billed as Leslie Parrish: *Portrait of a Mobster* (1961), *The Manchurian Candidate* (1962), *For Love or Money* (1963) and *Three on a Couch* (1966).

WITH ROBERT TAYLOR IN *TIP ON A DEAD JOCKEY*, 1958.

JOYCE JAMESON

Actually an intelligent and well-read lady, actress Joyce Jameson became the archetypical dumb blonde, because of her parts in films on television and the stage. She was born on September 26, 1932, in Chicago. Discovered in the revues and stage musicals by her first husband Billy Barnes, she came to Hollywood in 1950. After some bit parts she made a name for herself on national television (e.g. *The Abbott and Costello Show* and *The Steve Allen Show*). Her "Monroe connection" is the fact that she played Marilyn-type characters in various productions (e.g. in *The Billy Barnes Revue*, in director Billy Wilder's *The Apartment* [1960], dressed in Marilyn's black *Some Like it Hot* dress, and in 1962 she played the part of the MM-based character Olive Ogilvie in the Broadway play *Venus at Large*). Miss Jameson committed suicide on January 16, 1987. Some of her films: *Show Boat, The Strip* (both 1951), *Problem Girls* (1953), *Phffft!* (1954), *Gang Busters* (1955), *Crime Against Joe* and *Tension at Table Rock* (both 1956).

WITH BING CROSBY IN *HIGH SOCIETY*, 1956.

GRACE KELLY

Princess Grace of Monaco, who tragically died in a car crash in 1982, was a famous Hollywood star in the fifties. She was born Grace Patricia Kelly, in Philadelphia, on November 12, 1929. She started acting on the Broadway stage (1949's *The Father* and 1952's *To Be Continued)* and television and made her movie debut in 1951 in *Fourteen Hours*. Director Alfred Hitchcock used her for three of his suspense thrillers: *Dial M for Murder, Rear Window* (both 1954) and *To Catch a Thief* (1955). On loan from MGM to Paramount, she won an Oscar for Best Actress for her role in *The Country Girl* (1954). After *The Swan* and *High Society* (both 1956), she left Hollywood to start a new life as Princess Grace of Monaco. Grace Kelly's other films: *High Noon* (1952), *Mogambo* (1953), *Green Fire* and *The Bridges at Toko-Ri* (both 1954).

MARLON BRANDO WITH LARRI THOMAS, JUNE KIRBY AND PAT SHEEHAN IN *GUYS AND DOLLS*, 1955.

JUNE KIRBY

June Kirby was born in 1928, in New York. She was a showgirl at The Diamond Horseshoe nightclub in the late forties. She was spotted by MGM as a potential starlet and was offered a couple of film parts. In 1960 she left showbiz to marry Ray Whitlock in Los Angeles. Her film appearances include: *Kismet, Guys and Dolls* (both 1955), *The Garment Jungle* (1957), *The Last Hurrah* (1958) and *Bells are Ringing* (1960).

WITH VIC DAMONE IN *ATHENA*, 1954.

LUCY KNOCH

A Hollywood starlet since 1945, Lucy Knoch (born circa 1926) reached some fame on television when she was seen in *The Red Skelton Show* (1951). She was sometimes billed as Lucille Knox. In 1956 she was seen in a bit role in *Bus Stop*. She is mistaken by Don Murray for Marilyn Monroe. Earlier in her career she was also compared to Miss Monroe, with the small part she played in *Executive Suite* (1954), as the girlfriend of Louis Calhern, reminiscent of the part Monroe played opposite Calhern in *The Asphalt Jungle* (1950). Other films: *Incendiary Blonde* (1945), *The Blue Dahlia* (1946), *Welcome, Stranger* (1947), *The Big Clock* (1948), *Two Tickets to Broadway* (1951), *The Bad and the Beautiful* (1952), *The Clown, Sabre Jet, Half a Hero* (all 1953), *Athena* (1954), *Tennessee's Partner* (1955), *Anything Goes* (1956), *The Joker is Wild* (1957) and *The Buccaneer* (1958).

BARBARA LAWRENCE

Barbara Jo Lawrence was born on February 24, 1930, in Carnegie, Oklahoma. As a young girl she was a model, and in 1942 she was crowned "Little Miss Hollywood." She made her film debut in 1945 and studied acting at UCLA while appearing in bit parts under contract to 20th Century-Fox. She was married three times and retired in the early sixties from the movie business to sell real estate in Beverly Hills. Some of Miss Lawrence films: *Diamond Horseshoe* (1945), *Margie* (1946), *A Letter to Three Wives* (1948), *Peggy* (1950), *Two Tickets to Broadway* (1951), *Paris Model* (1953), *Man with the Gun* (1955), *Oklahoma!* (1955), *Kronos, Man in the Shadow* and *Joe Dakota* (all 1957).

LILA LEEDS

Lila Leeds was born Lila Lee Wilkinson on January 28, 1928, in Dodge City, Kansas. Miss Leeds is included in this book because she was a 1940s starlet who possibly would have made a career for herself in the fifties. We will never know how her career would have evolved because she had her notorious moment of fame when she was busted together with Robert Mitchum for smoking marihuana. Her career was damaged (Mitchum's wasn't) and she only starred in an exploitation film based on the event, *Wild Weed*, a.k.a. *She Shoulda Said No* (1949), before she vanished from the show business scene. Prior to her arrest she played in some films under contract to MGM and was called a threat to Lana Turner at the time. Films: *Lady in the Lake* (1947), *So You Want to be a Detective* (1948), *City Across the River* and *The House Across the Street* (both 1949). Married three times, Lila Leeds died on September 15, 1999.

JANET LEIGH

Jeanette Helen Morrison was born on July 6, 1927, in California. A screen test at MGM in 1947 led to a film contract. On June 5, 1954, she married actor Tony Curtis. Together, they starred in *Houdini* (1953), *The Black Shields of Falworth* (1954), *The Vikings* (1958), *The Perfect Furlough* (1958) and *Who Was That Lady?* (1960). With Curtis she had two daughters, Jamie Lee and Kelly (both became actresses). Director Alfred Hitchcock cast her in *Psycho* (1960), her most famous movie. For that role she was nominated for the Best Supporting Actress Academy Award. In 1962 she divorced Tony Curtis. She kept on acting until her death on October 3, 2004. Some of her other films: *Two Tickets to Broadway* (1951), *Living it Up* (1954), *Pete Kelly's Blues* (1955), *Safari* (1956), *Touch of Evil* (1958) and *Wives and Lovers* (1963).

MARA LYNN

Mara Lynn (Chicago, July 17, 1927) was a 5-foot-8-inch blonde of Swedish descent. She started out as a model and dancer in stage musicals (e.g. the Broadway musical *Inside U.S.A.*, April 30, 1948-February 19, 1949) before coming to Hollywood to appear in a couple of movies: *Prehistoric Women* (1950), *Leave it to the Marines*, *G.I. Jane* (both 1951), *Top Banana* (1954) and *Last Train from Gun Hill* (1959). Other Broadway musicals: *New Girl in Town* (May 1957-May 1958) and *The Body Beautiful* (January 1958-March 1958). Mara Lynn went on to a successful career as a dance director in Las Vegas. She was hired by Marilyn Monroe as dance coach for *Let's Make Love* (1960), and was also given a part in this movie. Mara Lynn died on April 6, 1988.

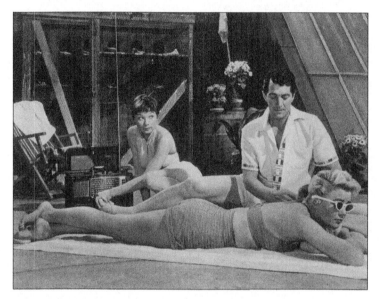

WITH SHIRLEY MACLAINE AND DEAN MARTIN IN *ARTISTS AND MODELS*, 1955.

DOROTHY MALONE

TV's *Peyton Place* actress Dorothy Malone was born Dorothy Eloise Maloney on January 30, 1925, in Chicago. She attended dancing classes from the age of three and later won several high school acting competitions. Originally a brunette, she made her debut in 1942 in *The Man Who Wouldn't Die*. She turned blonde for the Warner Bros. movie *Young at Heart* (1954) and remained that way for the rest of her career. She won an Oscar and a Golden Globe for her role in *Written on the Wind* (1956), playing Marylee Headly who is hopelessly in love with Rock Hudson. Among her other films: *The Big Sleep* (1946), *The Killer That Stalked New York* (1949), *Scared Stiff* (1953), *Pushover* (1954), *The Fast and the Furious,* (1955), *Pillars in the Sky* (1956), *Tip on a Dead Jockey, The Tarnished Angels* (both 1957), *Too Much, Too Soon* (1958), *Warlock* (1959) and *The Last Voyage* (1960).

THE FRIGHTENED CITY, 1961.

SHEENA MARSHE

Sheena Marshe (born in 1935) was a British fashion model who hit the news because she was a judoka trying to get into pictures. (She and husband Doug Robinson were partners in a London gymnasium.) Sheena made her movie debut in the Spanish/British co-production *Pasaporta al Infierno* (1956), in which she played a girl in the nightclub scenes. In Britain she was mostly seen in small television roles (e.g. *Educating Archie*, 1958) and commercials. In 1958 she landed an important role in the West End play *The Trial of Mary Dugan*, as a "know-all-about-men-girl." When Jayne Mansfield was making *The Sheriff of Fractured Jaw* (1958) in Britain, Sheena was considered as Jayne's stand-in, but Jayne wasn't pleased at all and the deal didn't come through. She appeared in the play *When in Rome* with June Laverick and Dickie Henderson, in 1959. Sheena Marshe did make some movies in the early sixties (*Over the Odds, Dentist on the Job, The Frightened City*, all 1961), but never reached real fame.

WITH DANA WYNTER IN *FRAULEIN*, 1958.

DOLORES MICHAELS

Dolores Michaels was originally trained in ballet. She worked as a dancer on Broadway, before going to Hollywood and signing a contract at 20th Century-Fox in 1957. She was born on January 30, 1933, in Kansas City, Missouri. In 1961 she married novelist and screenwriter Bernard Woolfe. Two years after her marriage, Dolores retired from show business. She was married to Woolfe until 1985 and the couple had two children. Dolores Michaels died on September 25, 2001, in West Hollywood, California. Some of her films: *The French Line* (1954), *Son of Sinbad* (1955), *The Wayward Bus, April Love* (both 1957), *The Fiend that Walked the West* (1958), *Warlock* and *Five Gates to Hell* (both 1959).

DIANA MUMBY (RIGHT) WITH BLONDE MARILYN MAXWELL IN *THE LEMON DROP KID*, 1951.

DIANA MUMBY

Starlet Diana (sometimes billed as Diane) Mumby was born in Detroit, Michigan, on July 1, 1922. She started her film career in 1940 in *A Night at Earl Carroll's*. She played a variety of cigarette girls, showgirls or chorines in forties and fifties musicals and comedies; she ended her career in 1956 with a small part in *The Harder They Fall*. Diane Mumby died on May 19, 1974, in Westlake, California. Some of the other films she appeared in: *The Kid from Brooklyn* (1946), *Winter Wonderland* (1947), *A Song is Born* (1948), *Air Hostess* (1949), *Beauty on Parade* (1950), *G.I. Jane* (1951), *The Las Vegas Story* (1952) and *Son of Sinbad* (1955).

WITH MAMIE VAN DOREN.

LORI NELSON

Pert, sometimes blonde Universal starlet Lori Nelson was born on August 18, 1933, in Santa Fe, New Mexico. At the age of four she moved to Hollywood and soon became "Miss Little America." At the age of seventeen she signed a seven-year contract with Universal. In January 1951 she was picked by the Hollywood make-up men as "Hollywood's most beautiful blonde." From 1957 'til 1958, she was one of the models (the others were Merry Anders and Barbara Eden) in TV's *How to Marry a Millionaire*. Some of Miss Nelson's movies: *Bend of the River* (1952), *All I Desire*, *The All American* (both 1953), *Destry* (1954), *Revenge of the Creature*, *Day the World Ended* (both 1955), *Hot Rod Girl* (1956), *Untamed Youth* (1957).

ANNE NEYLAND

Blonde pin-up/starlet Roberta Anne Neyland was born in Dallas around 1934. There she did some fashion modeling and appeared on local television, before going to Hollywood to appear in *Hidden Fear* (1957) with John Payne. That year she made two more films (*Jailhouse Rock* and *Motorcycle Gang*), then turned to television (*The Bob Cummings Show*, 1958 and *Richard Diamond, Private Detective*, 1959) and left Hollywood after a cameo in Frank Sinatra's *Ocean's Eleven* (1960) in the early sixties. During her short Hollywood career, Miss Neyland managed to land quite some publicity!

BETSY PALMER

Betsy Palmer was born Patricia Betsy Hrunek on November 1, 1926, in Chicago. She made her professional debut on television in 1951 and made her first movie in 1955. Betsy played her sexiest part in Columbia's *The True Story of Lynn Stuart* (1958). In 1954 she had married pediatrician Dr. Vincent Marandino. In 1962 their daughter Misy was born, but in 1971 the couple divorced. She only took the role of killer Jason's mother in chiller *Friday the 13th* (1980) because she needed the money to buy a car. It became the part she is best remembered for in her career! Other fifties films of Miss Palmer: *The Long Gray Line, Mister Roberts, Queen Bee* (all 1955), *The Tin Star* (1957) and *The Last Angry Man* (1959).

BARBARA PAYTON

This tragic blonde was a beautiful actress in the fifties, but too many scandals (with men mostly) ruined her career and led to drinking problems and prostitution. She was born Barbara Redfield on November 16, 1927, in Cloquet, Minnesota. In 1948 she went to Hollywood and was placed under contract by Universal. Having an affair at the same time with two men (actors Franchot Tone and Tom Neal), who fought a public brawl over her, damaged her film career. She made a couple of movies in Great Britain and disappeared from the movie scene in 1955. She wrote her autobiography *I Am Not Ashamed!* in 1963. On May 8, 1967, she died from heart and liver failure; she was 39 years old. Some of her movies: *Once More, My Darling, Trapped* (both 1949), *Kiss Tomorrow Goodbye, Dallas* (both 1950), *Bride of the Gorilla* (1951), *Four Sided Triangle, The Great Jesse James Raid* (both 1953) and *Murder is My Beat* (1955).

On the magazine cover:

Picturegoer

THE NATIONAL FILM AND ENTERTAINMENT WEEKLY

EVERY THURSDAY

4°

I LEARNED MY LESSON

BY FRANKIE VAUGHAN

STOP THESE TV SHOCKS

DORS writes from Hollywood

UNA PEARL —she's standing in for Monroe

UNA PEARL

British Una Pearl (real name Pearl King, 1935) was the stand-in for both Marilyn Monroe (in *The Prince and the Sho*wgirl, 1957) and France's number one blonde, Brigitte Bardot (in *Babette s'en va–'t en Guerre*, 1959). She played some small parts in *An Alligator Named Daisy* (1955) and *The Silken Affair* (1956). Una Pearl retired from show business in the sixties to raise her children.

WITH ROCK HUDSON IN *THIS EARTH IS MINE*, 1959.

CINDY ROBBINS

Cindy Robbins was born in Hammond, Louisiana, on January 5, 1937. In 1957 she made her film debut in *I Was a Teenage Werewolf* (1957). Shortly after her 19th birthday, she gave birth to a daughter; Kimberly Beck, who also became an actress. The press sometimes referred to her as "Hollywood's answer to Brigitte Bardot." In 1960 she was nominated for the Golden Laurel award for being one of the most promising female stars of the year. In the mid-sixties she stopped acting, and briefly lived in Australia with her daughter and new husband, singer/ actor Tommy Leonetti. Cindy's other films: *Dino, Gunsight Ridge, Rockabilly Baby* (all 1957), *This Earth is Mine* (1959).

WITH CARLA MEREY AND JUDY BAMBER IN *DRAGSTRIP GIRL*, 1957.

FAY SPAIN

Fay Spain was born Lona Fay Spain, on October 6, 1932, in Phoenix, Arizona. Together with Roxanne Arlen and a dozen other starlets she was chosen as one of the WAMPAS Baby Stars of 1956. She lost a role in *The Sharkfighters* (1956) to Karen Steele, and appeared in a couple of television shows that same year. In 1957 she made her film debut in director Roger Corman's *Dragstrip Girl*, but she emerged from the B-features in *God's Little Acre* (1958), playing Robert Ryan's tempting daughter. Some of her other movies are: *Teenage Doll* (1957), *The Beat Generation, Al Capone* (both 1959) and *The Private Lives of Adam and Eve* (1960). Fay Spain died of cancer on May 8, 1983 in Los Angeles.

JAN STERLING

She was born Jane Sterling Adriance, on April 3, 1923, in New York City. She made her movie debut under the name of Jane Adrian in *Tycoon* in 1947, and thereafter was known as Jan Sterling. Her second marriage was to actor Paul Douglas, from 1950 'til his death in 1959. She was nominated for an Academy Award for her part in *The High and the Mighty* (1954). Her sexy dance in *The Human Jungle* (1954) was banned by some censors. In *The Police Dog Story* (1956), she also did a striptease routine. Jan Sterling's other films include: *Caged* (1950), *Rhubarb* (1951), *Flesh and Fury* (1952), *Split Second* (1953), *Women's Prison* (1955), *The Harder They Fall* (1956), *Slaughter on Tenth Avenue* (1957), *High School Confidential!* (1958) and *Love in a Goldfish Bowl* (1961).

ANGELA STEVENS

Angela Stevens was born on May 8, 1925. She started her film career under the name of Ann Zita (her husband's name). She was a model for photographer Tom Kelley (who shot the famous nude photos of Marilyn Monroe in the late forties). After many small parts, she received star billing in a couple of B-movies in the mid-fifties and quit acting in the early sixties to take care of her 15-year-old son, who had broken his neck after diving on a sandbar. Some of Miss Stevens' films: *Tea For Two* (1950), *Two Tickets to Broadway* (1951), *Eight Iron Men* (1952), *The Wild One* (1953), *The Last Time I Saw Paris* (1954), *Women's Prison, Creature with the Atomic Brain, Devil Goddess* (all 1955), *Blackjack Ketchum, Desperado* (1956), *Utah Blaine* (1957) and *Triple Crossed* (1959).

INGER STEVENS

Swedish-born Inger Stensland (born on August 18, 1934, in Stockholm, Sweden) came to the United States with her father (her parents were divorced) in 1947. At sixteen she ran away from home and eventually became a student at Lee Strasberg's Actors' Studio in New York. She played on television and on Broadway before going to Hollywood in 1957. She had a hard time in the mid-sixties when it became public that she had married a black man. On April 30, 1970, Inger Stevens committed suicide with sleeping pills. Her films include: *Man on Fire* (1957), *Cry Terror, The Buccaneer* (both 1958), *The World, the Flesh and the Devil* (1959), *The New Interns* (1964), *A Guide for the Married Man* (1967) and *Madigan* (1968).

STELLA STEVENS

Stella Stevens was born Estelle Caro Eggleston, on October 1, 1936 and is probably the last of the blonde bombshells who started her career in the late fifties. On the threshold of the sixties Stella appeared in three movies (*Say One for Me, The Blue Angel* and *L'il Abner*, all 1959) and had a nude layout in *Playboy* in January 1960. She was expected to take over the crown when Marilyn Monroe died in 1962. Of course, the decade of sexy dumb blondes died with Monroe, but Stella had a nice film career in the sixties. Some of her sixties films: *Too Late Blues* (1961), *Girls! Girls! Girls!* (1962), *The Nutty Professor* (1963), *The Silencers* (1966).

LARRI THOMAS

Larri Thomas was born Linda Larrimore Thomas on January 23, 1932, in Wayne, Pennsylvania. She was a Hollywood starlet/dancer in the fifties. Larri was one of the three blonde Goldwyn Girls (the others were June Kirby and Pat Sheehan) who helped promote MGM's *Guys and Dolls* (1955) in New York. In December 1955 she married actor John Bromfield. Larri had a small role as a dancer in his *Curucu, Beast of the Amazon* (1956). The couple divorced in 1959. Other films: *Million Dollar Mermaid* (1952), *Here Come the Girls* (1953), *Rails into Laramie* (1954), *Love Me or Leave Me, Artists and Models* (both 1955), *The Best Things in Life are Free* (1956), *The Pajama Game* (1957), *South Pacific* (1958), *Ask Any Girl, The Beat Generation* (both 1959), *Who Was That Lady?* (1960), *The Music Man* (1962), *Island of Love* (1963), *Robin and the 7 Hoods, Mary Poppins* (both 1964), *The Silencers* and *Frankie and Johnny* (both 1966).

GRETA THYSSEN

Pin-up girl Greta Thyssen (née Thysegen) was born in Copenhagen, Denmark in 1931. She became Miss Denmark in 1951. She left for Hollywood soon thereafter and she was referred to as "The Danish answer to Marilyn Monroe." Mostly seen on television, Greta made her debut as a cover girl in Monroe's *Bus Stop* (1956). She was seen in a couple of The Three Stooges' shorts (*Pies and Guys*, 1958 and *Sappy Bullfighters*, 1959). A few cheap thrillers and dramas followed: *Accused of Murder* (1956), *The Beast from Budapest* (1958), *Terror is a Man, Catch Me If You Can* and *Shadows* (all 1959), *Three Blondes in His Life* (1961), *Journey to the Seventh Planet* (1962), *The Double-Barrelled Detective Story* (1965). All was ended in style with the awful *Cottonpickin' Chickenpickers* (1967).

HAPPY ANNIVERSARY, 1959.

MONIQUE VAN VOOREN

Belgian-born Monique van Vooren (March 23, 1925) came to Hollywood in 1952. In Europe she was a famous junior ice skating champion. She made films in Europe and in the US. In the US she also toured the country with plays (e.g. the Broadway musical revue *John Murray Anderson's Almanac*, 1953-1954 and *Destry Rides Again*, 1961) and singing in cabaret. Her nickname was "The Belgian Bulge." Some films: *Domani è Tropo Tardi/Tomorrow is Too Late* (1949), *Tarzan and the She-Devil* (1953), *Ça va Barder* (1955), *Ten Thousand Bedrooms* (1957), *Gigi* (1958), *Happy Anniversary* (1959), *Fearless Frank* (1969), *Flesh for Frankenstein* (1973).

WITH MARA LYNN AND JOHANN PETURSSON IN
PREHISTORIC WOMEN, **1950.**

KERRY VAUGHN

Kerry Vaughn (born in 1925) made a name for herself in showbiz by appearing in the now-cult classic *Prehistoric Women* (1950) and marrying famous singer Tony Fontane on May 2, 1950. She was a Universal starlet in the mid-forties, when she was also shortly married to actor Peter Coe. For a while she was Lana Turner's stand-in. Together with Fontane she toured through Australia in the early fifties with the stage musicals *Show Boat* and *Zip Goes a Million*, and became hugely popular there. She was even called "The Australian Monroe." The Fontanes had one child, Char Fontane (born 1952). She also became an actress, and died recently on April 1, 2007. Kerry Vaughn Fontane died in 1996 from cancer. Some of her films: *Atlantic City* (1944), *Salome Where She Danced* (1945), *A Night in Paradise* (1946), *Excuse My Dust* (1951), *Something to Live For* (1952), *The Ten Commandments* (1956) and *The Tony Fontane Story* (1963).

WITH BRUCE BENNETT IN *FIEND OF DOPE ISLAND*, 1961.

TANIA VELIA

This former Miss Yugoslavia (born on February 11, 1934) competed in the 1954 Olympic Games as part of the Yugoslavian swimming team, before she came to the US to appear in *Queen of Outer Space* (1958), *Missile to the Moon* (1959) and *Fiend of Dope Island* (1961). In the latter she plays dancer/entertainer Glory LaVerne and has a nude swimming scene. When her film career ended she went to New York where she had a small role in the Broadway play *A Call on Kuprin* (1961). In the mid-sixties she settled in Spain.

YVETTE VICKERS

This *Playboy* Playmate of the Month, July 1959, was born Yvette Vedder on August 26, 1935, in Kansas City, Missouri. Only 14 years old, she landed her first movie part, in Billy Wilders' *Sunset Blvd.* as one of the giggly girls on the telephone in the party scene. She was nasty to Gloria Castillo as juvenile delinquent Roxy in *Reform School Girl* (1957) and made an everlasting impression on moviegoers in the cult picture *Attack of the 50 Foot Woman* (1958). As Honey Parker, she's fooling around with Allison Hayes' husband. Other small parts in B-movies and a lot of television appearances rounded out the fifties. Some films: *The Sad Sack* (1957), *I Mobster, Juvenile Jungle* (both 1958), *Attack of the Giant Leeches* (1959), *Hud* and *Beach Party* (both 1963).

JEAN WALLACE

Earl Carroll's and Ziegfeld Follies chorine Jean Walasek was born on October 12, 1923, in Chicago, Illinois. At age eighteen she made her movie debut and married actor Franchot Tone. (In 1948 they divorced.) She attempted suicide in 1946 with sleeping pills, and in 1949 with a self-inflicted knife wound. In 1951 she married an actor again. Together with actor/husband Cornel Wilde she starred in *Star of India* (1954) *The Big Combo, Storm Fear* (both 1955), *The Devil's Hairpin* (1957), *Maracaibo* (1958), *Lancelot and Guinevere* (1963) and *Beach Red* (1967). After thirty years of marriage, she divorced Wilde. Jean Wallace died on February 14, 1990, in Beverly Hills. Other films: *Blaze of Noon* (1947), *Jigsaw* (1949), *The Man on the Eiffel Tower* and *The Good Humor Man* (both 1950).

WITH GARY VINSON IN *ROCKABILLY BABY*, 1957.

SANDRA WIRTH

Sandra Wirth (sometimes billed as Sandy Wirth) was Miss Florida in 1955, which led to film work and television. She was born around 1934. Her first assignment after the beauty competition was when she was cast as a semi-regular on the popular Sunday afternoon kid TV show *Super Circus* (1955) at ABC. *A Face in the Crowd, Forty Guns, Rockabilly Baby* (all 1957), *The Naked and the Dead* (1958) and *Missile to the Moon* (1959) were some of the films in which she played.

"BYE BYE, BABY!" (SANDRA WIRTH).

BIBLIOGRAPHY

Baker, Carroll. *Baby Doll*. New York: Dell Publishing Co., Inc., 1985.

Betrock, Alan. *Battle of the Blondes — Jayne Mansfield vs Mamie Van Doren*. New York: Shake Books, 1993.

Betrock, Alan. *The I was a Teenage Juvenile Delinquent Rock 'n' roll Horror Beach Party Movie Book*. London: Plexus Publishing Limited, 1986.

Brode, Douglas. *Lost Films of the Fifties*. Secaucus, N.J.: Citadel Press, 1988.

Cameron, Ian and Elisabeth. *Dames*. New York: Frederick A. Praeger, Inc., Publishers, 1969.

Cross, Robin. *The Big Book of British Films*. London: Charles Herridge Ltd., 1984.

Dimmitt, Richard Bertrand. *An Actor Guide to the Talkies*. Metuchen, N.J.: Scarecrow Press, 1967.

Doherty, Thomas: *Teenagers & Teenpics — The Juvenilization of American Movies in the 1950s*. London: Unwin Hyman Ltd., 1988.

Dors, Diana. *Behind Closed Dors*. London: W. H. Allen, 1979.

Dors, Diana. *Dors by Diana — an intimate self-portrait*. London: Futura Publications, 1983.

Dors, Diana. *Swingin' Dors*. London: WDL, 1960.

Duca, Lo. *Die Erotik im Film — Die Welt des Eros*. Basel: Verlag Kurt Desch, 1965.

Eaton, Shirley. *Golden Girl*. London: B. T. Batsford Ltd., 1999.

Faris, Jocelyn. *Jayne Mansfield — a Bio-Bibliography*. Westport: Greenwood Press, 1994.

Feeney Callan, Michael. *Pink Goddess — The Jayne Mansfield Story*. London: W. H. Allen, 1986.

Ferruccio, Frank. *Diamonds to Dust, The Life and Death of Jayne Mansfield*. Denver: Outskirts Press, Inc., 2007.

Gifford, Dennis. *The British Film Catalogue 1895-1985*. London: Davis & Charles, 1986.

James, Brandon. *Jeanne Carmen — My Wild, Wild Life*. Lincoln: iUniverse, Inc., 2006.

Kleno, Larry. *Kim Novak on Camera*. New York: A. S. Barnes & Company, Inc., 1980.

Koper, Richard. *Dreamgirl — The Films of Joi Lansing*. San Francisco: Blurb.com, 2008.

Koper, Richard. *Blonde Broad — The Films of Barbara Nichols*. San Francisco: Blurb.com, 2010.

Krasna, Norman. *Who was that lady I saw you with?* New York: Random House, 1958.

Lowe, Barry. *Atomic Blonde - The Films of Mamie Van Doren.* Jefferson: McFarland & Company, Inc, Publishers, 2008.

Lloyd, Ann and Robinson, David. *Movies of the Fifties.* London: Orbis Publishing Limited, 1984.

Mansfield, Jayne and Hargitay, Mickey. *Jayne Mansfield's Wild, Wild World.* Los Angeles: Holoway House Publishing Company, 1963

Martin, Len D. *The Allied Artists Checklist. The feature films and short subjects, 1947-1978.* Jefferson: McFarland & Company, Inc., Publishers, 1993.

Martin, Pete. *Will acting spoil Marilyn Monroe?* New York: Cardinal, 1957.

McGee, Mark Thomas. *The Rock and Roll Movie Encyclopedia of the 1950s.* Jefferson: McFarland & Company, Inc., Publishers, 1990.

McGee, Mark Thomas. *Roger Corman — The Best of the Cheap Acts.* Jefferson: McFarland & Company, Inc., Publishers, 1988.

Milner, Michael. *Sex on Celluloid.* New York: MacFadden Books, 1964.

Parish, James Robert. *The Fox Girls.* ?: Arlington House Publishers, Inc., 1972.

Parish, James Robert and Stanke, Don E. *The Glamour Girls.* Carlstadt, New Jersey: Rainbow Books, 1977.

Pascall, Jeremy and Jeavons, Clyde. *A Pictorial History of Sex in the Movies.* London: The Hamlyn Publishing Group Limited, 1975.

Quinlan, David. *Wicked Women of the Screen.* London: B.T. Batford Ltd., 1987.

Riese, Randall and Hitchens, Neal. *The Unabridged Marilyn — Her Life from A to Z.* New York: Congdon & Weed, Inc. 1987.

Saxton, Martha. *Jayne Mansfield and the American Fifties.* Boston: Houghton Mifflin Company, 1975.

Sullivan, Steve. *Bombshells.* New York: St. Martin's Press, 1998.

Sullivan, Steve. *Glamour Girls — The Illustrated Encyclopedia.* New York: St. Martin's Press, 1999.

Sullivan, Steve. *Va Va Voom — Bombshells, Pin-ups, Sexpots and Glamour Girls.* Los Angeles: General Publishing Group, 1995.

Van Doren, Mamie. *I Swing.* New York: Novel Books, 1965.

Van Doren, Mamie and Aveilhe, Art. *Playing the Field — My Story.* New York: G. P. Putnam's Sons, 1987.

Victor, Adam. *The Marilyn Encyclopedia.* Woodstock, New York: Peter Mayer Publishers, Inc., 1999.

Wise, Damon. *Come by Sunday — the fabulous, ruined life of Diana Dors.* London: Pan Books, 1999.

Recommended website: *www.glamourgirlsofthesilverscreen.com,* by my collector friend Robert Rotter.

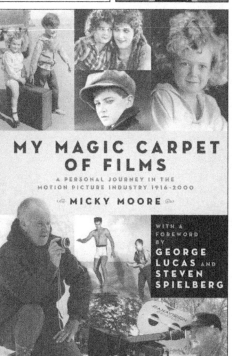
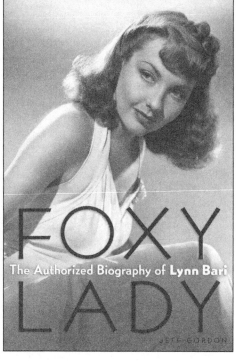

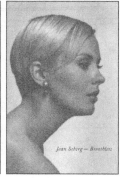

Printed in Great Britain
by Amazon

86293363R00231